THE
UNBROKEN ME
A Woman's Journey from
Feeling Unfulfilled to
Finding True Freedom

KRISTINE BOLT

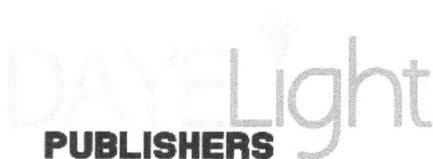

DayeLight PUBLISHERS

ISBN: 978-1-958443-84-2 (paperback)

For every woman who feels unfulfilled, and misunderstood because of it. I see you, girl, and so does God.

ACKNOWLEDGMENTS

I wrote this book, but it wouldn't exist without a few special people.

Kim Lucretia, who first planted the idea of this book in my mind and who wouldn't let it go, even when I resisted.

Shamena Khan, in whose sanctuary of kindness, generosity, and love most of this book came together, and who has always believed in big things for me.

Meila McKitty-Plummer, a confident, on-purpose woman who stuck with me when I became a pariah, and who inspires me to keep growing as a confident, on-purpose woman myself.

A girl couldn't ask for a better cheer squad at her back. Thank You, God, for them, and for anointing me to write this book.

TABLE OF CONTENTS

Preface 9

1. In the Valley of Discontent and Despair.......................13

2. Trapped by Idols...19

3. The Slide to Rock Bottom...31

4. The Peace of God (And a Whole Lot More)..................43

5. Hitting Reset...53

6. Get Up and Go...61

7. "I Love You" 71

8. Healing, Healing, and More Healing 81

9. A Whole New World 97

10. Freedom..105

Individual Reflection or Book Club Discussion Questions
....111

About the Author..127

Thank You for Reading! 129

PREFACE

In February 2017, I gave a speech at a service club for young professionals that was positively terrible—the speech, not the club.

About two years before, they had invited me to give a motivational talk about the upheaval in my life over the preceding year or so. My first visit with the club members went well, so they invited me back for part two of the speech. I was to talk about how my life had changed since then.

I figured it wouldn't be too hard, so I put together a slideshow with pictures from the time since I'd last spoken to the club. I intended to discuss how I'd gotten to this point, my experiences during the intervening period, and what I'd learned so far.

When it was time to speak, I was ready to knock their socks off with stories of my amazing adventures.

Instead, my presentation flopped, and my audience wasn't at all impressed.

Throughout my twenty-minute talk, almost every one of them stared sightlessly at my slides. I got zero interest, energy, or engagement from them, and it was pretty obvious that they wished I'd hurry up and finish already.

Still, I powered through and tried to deliver my underlying message: change can feel hard, but embracing it can be the most rewarding experience of your life.

They cared not one whit.

When my time was over, they thanked me and gave me a certificate of appreciation for my positively awful speech.

On my way out of the meeting, I fumed over these clueless twenty-somethings' lack of appreciation for my extraordinary journey over the previous few years. Clearly, they didn't understand the opportunity they'd been gifted to learn something great from me.

But by the time I drove away a couple of minutes later, I'd climbed down off my high horse and admitted the truth to myself: my talk had come off like an extended boast instead of as a testimony to God's grace and mercy in my life.

The truth was, a service club of up-and-coming young professionals whose main goal was to accomplish and acquire the things I'd left behind wasn't the right audience for my story.

What did they care about feeling resentful but desperate to hang on to an unfulfilling, well-paying job? Or about feeling trapped by their responsibilities and obligations? Or about being down to their last shred of hope that God would *finally* answer their panicked pleas for rescue?

They didn't. But you do.

You care about living free from the chains of fear and guilt. You care about keeping your faith in God's promises to you and your faith in yourself. And you care about having enough courage to step into God's will for your life, despite your bank account, age, relationship status, or past missteps.

This was the stuff I cared about too when I was exactly where you are now—feeling unfulfilled and stuck in your current circumstances, scared to leave them, confused about your next step, and unheard by God through it all.

Let my story stand as a witness to what's possible for you because God is extending to you the same hand of amazing, saving grace that He extended to me.

Learn what it looks like to kick unfulfillment to the curb, step into God's plan and purpose for you, and walk in a level of freedom you never knew existed.

> *Jesus said to the people who believed in him, "You are truly my disciples if you remain faithful to my teachings. And you will know the truth, and the truth will set you free." John 8:31-32 NLT*

GET A FREE DOWNLOAD

I have a gift for you!

It's a free, exclusive prayer companion that goes along with this book. It has a Bible verse and a prayer prompt for each chapter and section in this book, so you can pray as you journey with me from feeling unfulfilled to finding true freedom.

To get it, all you need to do is:

1. Go to signup.kristinebolt.com/unbroken-prayer-companion.
2. Enter your email address.
3. Less than 10 seconds later, check your inbox for your free exclusive companion download.

Now, let's go!

I

IN THE VALLEY OF DISCONTENT AND DESPAIR

From the depths of despair, O Lord, I call for your help. Hear my cry, O Lord. Pay attention to my prayer. Psalm 130:1-2 NLT

When I was a kid, I believed I was special to God. I remember with crystal clarity being 4 or 5 years old and playing one day in the shadow of a bush at the side of our house. Suddenly, out of nowhere, a feeling of certainty and confidence that I was special to God washed over me like a wave. It was the first time I'd ever felt physically wrapped in His love, and the experience knocked the wind out of me. I crouched next to the bush, stunned and still, as I let myself be overwhelmed with joy and delight. It was a quick, pleasantly heavy moment. Then I went back to playing by the bush.

For years after those precious few seconds, my future was sort of fuzzy and vague, but I knew without a doubt that God had special plans for my life. Thinking about it never failed

13

to break me out in goosebumps of excitement and anticipation.

By the time I hit my teenage years, I still felt special and assumed I'd have a fulfilling life—one brimming with purpose and meaning, one where I'd make a big difference in other people's lives. I had visions of traveling the earth doing a vague, fuzzy something that would impact lives, fulfill me, and make me Croesus-level rich.

But my mid-thirties brought a different reality. By then, I felt like a regular woman living a regular life. Sure, I made good money and had checked the boxes of what the world said was success, but I hadn't done anything extraordinary. I was just one of 8 billion people in the world. Who could tell me apart from the people in my neighborhood, much less from 8 billion people? As far as I was concerned, no one could be special among 8 billion people, even to God. On top of that, God hadn't said a word to me in *years*. Besides—begging, pleading, and bruised knees, aside—when someone is special to you, you don't ignore them, right? And by then, I felt well and truly ignored by God.

This was how, without me even noticing, I gradually let go of my childhood belief that I was special to God. It was as if my moment by the bush in the yard had never happened.

THE TRUTH UNDER THE LIE

Back in May 2014, my life looked golden. I was a young vice president in a large, publicly listed corporation in my home country of Jamaica. I was in a long-term, committed relationship with a popular, charming man who I deeply loved. We lived together in our renovated house on the hill, with my luxury car parked in the driveway. And you could have stocked a small boutique from my walk-in closet. My life was a beautiful portrait of success and happiness. Except, it was all a lie.

I hated my job. My self-esteem was in tatters because of the relationship. You could have sliced through the tension inside my gorgeous house with a rusty spoon. And the amount of money I hemorrhaged trying to keep that darn car roadworthy could have fed a small family for months. My life was the definition of secret misery and dissatisfaction.

Let's start with the job. It paid really well but, by then, I abhorred it and felt trapped in it. This was mainly because I'd been trying for years to figure out what God wanted me to do with my life, but I still had no clue. Even if I left my job, I reasoned, I didn't know what to do with myself that wouldn't have me feeling trapped all over again.

Then there was the relationship. My partner didn't let an opportunity pass to make me feel unworthy of him, and I didn't have the courage or self-awareness to choose better for myself. So I spent most of my time at home living in a state of constant tension, feeling like I wasn't good enough for him every second of every day, trying—and failing—to be the woman he said I needed to be.

In the middle of my mess, I cried out to God—had been for *years*—begging Him to rescue me, make my situation better, and make me happy again. But He seemed silent and I felt unheard by Him. So, I decided to take matters into my own hands and try to fix my unhappiness myself.

As a hardworking, high-achieving woman, I left no stone unturned in my search for a solution. I devoured the latest self-help books, eager for the secret to a life of bliss. I went to counseling, hoping they would give me the answer to my question about why, with all I'd accomplished, I felt unfulfilled. I tried new hobbies, hoping they would fulfill my desire for satisfaction since nothing else in my life did. I volunteered in a couple of ministries at my church, with my fingers crossed that focusing on those less fortunate than I was would kill my discontent with my life.

I watched TED talks and *Super Soul Sunday*, waiting in anticipation for the "aha!" moment when I would hear something that would turn things around for me. I went to weekend Christian conferences and returned from them feeling slightly better, but not for more than a couple of days. I repeated affirmations daily, trying and failing to convince myself that "I am perfectly whole and complete."

Oh, and the gratitude jar! I kept it on my nightstand, along with cute little patterned slips of paper and a pink pen. Every night before bed, I was supposed to jot down one thing I was grateful for that day. I wasn't allowed to reuse what I'd written on previous days, and I couldn't write basic stuff, like food, shelter, and clothes. And do you know what? Most nights, I couldn't think of even one thing to write. Not one.

It wasn't that I wasn't grateful for the roof over my head, the food in my fridge, the clothes on my back, or the money in my bank account. It was more that those things didn't feel like…well, *enough.*

But the life I'd created was good, and I felt like an ungrateful jerk for feeling restless and dissatisfied with it. So, I used the gratitude jar as a tool to shame myself into believing that my life was perfectly fine and I shouldn't be miserable. I didn't know then that my dissatisfaction and disquiet were symptoms of a deeper issue. I also didn't know that God was using them as a set-up for snatching me out of the great-looking life I'd built on a foundation of wrong choices.

And so, like all the other things I tried to fix my unhappiness, the gratitude jar failed miserably. In fact, every single thing I tried only deepened my despair because they seemed to work for others but not for me.

I remember standing at my office window, staring out over the rain-soaked business district below, wondering how much longer I could hang on. This had become a habit—standing at my office window, locked in a battle with myself, feeling defeated, lost, and panicked about how to fix my despair.

Kristine Bolt

"Maybe," I thought, "I should forget about a meaningful life and just do whatever the heck I want." It seemed to work for everyone else; their social media highlight reels said so. Except, something deep inside me screamed that I *wasn't* everyone else, and it wouldn't let me release my desire for more.

Eventually, I found myself in a place where I felt alone and abandoned—by the job I used to love, the partner who claimed to love me, and God, who seemed not to love me anymore. No wonder I felt unfulfilled and unhappy!

The funny thing was, even though by then I felt like my problems didn't matter to God, I still kept up my desperate prayers: begging Him every day to zap me with happiness so I wouldn't feel miserable anymore, fervently hoping for a miraculous turnaround; frantically wishing on my Bible to stop feeling ungrateful because, really, what did I have to be so unhappy about? My life looked great!

As it turned out, God had heard me all along. He'd answered my desperate prayers, but I didn't notice until He stripped me of almost everything I'd achieved. That was when I allowed Him to expose the truth, rescue me from the trap of a life I'd created, lead me into my next step, and remind me of how special I'd always been to Him.

2

TRAPPED BY IDOLS

But be careful. Don't let your heart be deceived so that you turn away from the Lord and serve and worship other gods.
Deuteronomy 11:16 NLT

My eyes were still closed as I surfaced through the last layers of sleep into awareness. I heard the world waking up outside my window and felt the soft sunlight on my eyelids. It was morning. I did a quick mental check of what day it was and sighed in relief when I realized my alarm hadn't woken me, so it must not be a workday. Suddenly, I didn't give a hoot anymore what day it was, as long as it wasn't a workday.

Another sigh of relief slipped out at the thought that I didn't need to steel my emotions or draw on my mental reserves to deal with the mere thought of going to work. Then I rolled my now-open eyes at myself. My attitude seemed ungrateful since I knew lots of people would die to be in my position, earning what I was. Plus, it never used to be this way—I used to *love* my work.

To be honest, I was kinda sick of myself for my circular thoughts about my job—one moment telling myself I should be grateful, the next moment wondering if I would ever find the purpose and meaning I wanted from it, the next feeling resentful because I didn't see how I could leave it, then back to telling myself I should be grateful. At first, I figured this was just a phase, but it had lasted way too long and I was starting to panic. If I didn't get over it soon, my boss and colleagues would be on to me.

By the time 2014 rolled around, I'd been in that particular corporate executive job for almost five years. It was in the last two of those years that—besides wanting to hide under the covers on workdays—I'd gotten into the habit of staring blindly out my high-rise office window.

I think anyone looking at me standing by the window would have assumed that I was contemplating my next monthly report, working out a strategy for dealing with that one toxic person poisoning my whole team, or planning a countermove to stop my backstabbing colleague from passing off my hard work as his. But I wasn't. As sick and tired as I was of the corporate politics and drama, my window-staring time was spent wondering what all my hard work was for and trying to figure out how to stop feeling so miserable at my job.

For a large part of my corporate career, money—the company's bottom line and my compensation package—had driven me from my bed every morning; it was my idol. But suddenly, money didn't feel like a good enough motivator anymore. Still, as miserable as I was at work, the money, perks, and status were so good that I couldn't give them up. The people I knew back then would have laughed me out of town if I'd done that.

Speaking of whom, it seemed like no one in my life got why I felt so unsettled. They didn't understand my desire for deeper purpose and meaning. Their advice fell into one of two camps. One camp told me to get a regular dose of fulfillment by focusing on the less fortunate. The other camp said I should count my blessings—hence, the gratitude jar that taunted me from my nightstand. Looking back, I think most of them meant well, but I always walked away from those conversations feeling low-key ungrateful and ashamed.

I sought answers in books about parachutes, in career quizzes that promised to point me towards work that should fulfill me, and in personality tests that were supposed to tell me how to use my strengths and weaknesses to my advantage in all areas of my life, including my work.

I thought about changing jobs for a fresh challenge; maybe that would bring joy back to my work. But moving to another corporation to work for *their* bottom line and to navigate *their* politics and drama wasn't appealing. As confused as I was about what to do, I didn't need anyone to tell me one simple truth: the problem wasn't my employer; the problem was inside me.

I'd have loved to take a gap year then. But I felt trapped by my financial commitments—car payments, mortgage, groceries, utilities, funding my lifestyle and my retirement account. *I was being responsible,* I told myself. Besides, I was almost two decades too late to go off and "find myself."

My partner knew how unhappy I was, and he encouraged me to hang on to my job by fueling myself with outside activities that I enjoyed. To be honest, though, I only wanted to explore faraway places, which looked nigh on impossible. Our travel consisted of going to the same tired places over and over, and the type of travel I dreamed about seemed far out of my reach. So I bit my tongue, sucked it up, and stayed trapped in my high-rise office.

Meanwhile, every day, I sank deeper into misery, dragged under by my desire to keep making the big bucks. Something had to give, and I didn't know it yet, but that something was me.

THE SHADOW I BECAME

After dragging myself through each day at the job I hated, I dragged myself through my evenings, working at my dining table as an unpaid employee in my partner's company. I hated that job too, but I thought not helping him would be selfish and unsupportive. So I gritted my teeth and burned the midnight oil. Besides that, years of battering from his constant criticism meant I'd swallowed the lie—hook, line, and sinker—that I never measured up. By then, I genuinely believed I didn't deserve better and thought I was lucky that this man was willing to bear the burden of being in a relationship with me.

"What's wrong with you? No other woman I know would ever do that."

"All you've done is teach me patience. Otherwise, I couldn't have dealt with you all this time."

"I don't even know why I love you anymore."

He said all this and more to me, and I swallowed all of it. Eventually, most of my emotional energy went into forcing myself into the mold he'd created for me. I prayed every morning that today would be the day I was finally good enough for him.

Of course, our relationship didn't start out that way. Initially, I was a reasonably confident woman who thought I deserved a good man. But ten years of having your identity and self-worth undermined can erode even the strongest sense of self.

I remember the time he called me an "attention whore." The instant the words left his mouth, my jaw dropped and my eyes almost bulged out of my head. Time slowed to a crawl as my brain tried to understand what I'd just heard, and then it sped right up again as a roaring filled my ears. Nobody had ever called me a whore of any sort in my entire life, and

I didn't know how to process it, especially since it came from the person who claimed to love me above all others.

With frustrated tears trembling on my lashes, my words of defense and outrage tripped over themselves, trying to spill from my mouth. But, as my whole body seemed to throb with pain from the wound he'd just inflicted, all that came out was a tangled mass of half-thoughts and unfinished sentences. I could tell he'd been hanging on to that one for a while. It was obvious once he started listing the reasons why he'd decided I was an attention whore. I was a hugger, which he said made me look loose. I did too much for my friends, which he said somehow devalued the things I did for him. I laughed too loudly, which he said made me seem vulgar and desperate for the spotlight. He turned my good qualities into something sordid and weaponized them, and I let him use them to destroy my self-worth and self-image. Even worse, that particular verbal beat-down ended with me—feeling dirty and cheap—finally agreeing that I was an attention whore. Except, I didn't actually think I was.

Sadly, most of our conversations ended that way, with me crumbling under the pressure of his unstoppable logic. This wasn't surprising since I'd slowly let him turn me into a quivering mass of insecurity, convinced that he knew me better than I knew myself.

Then there was the time he called me a selfish, deceitful psychopath, after which he straight-up said I was the worst woman he knew. Why? Because I'd made a will and hadn't told him about it, and because I'd been saving money from my paycheck every month and had deliberately hidden it from him.

Why had I done those things? Because, by then, I didn't trust him with money. Because I was afraid of where we'd end up if I kept giving him wads of cash to go out and gamble away several nights each week. And because wisdom said I should do what was necessary to prepare for our financial future, despite his bad habits. It all came out unexpectedly one evening, which was when he hurled his "You're a psychopath!" accusation at me. I wasn't expecting the direct hit, so I didn't have time to shield my heart. In an instant, my world tilted off its axis and didn't straighten up again for weeks. I thought—hoped—he was speaking in anger and frustration. After all, he'd spent literal *hours* dissecting every one of my faults that he could tie to my financial deception and even some that he couldn't.

But I was wrong.

He was so serious that he threw his accusations in my face countless times during the next few days. Maybe he did it so I wouldn't forget, kind of like how some people rub a puppy's nose in its poop as a way of disciplining it. Or maybe he did it so I'd know he wasn't kidding, that I needed to get my act together this time and finally be the woman he wanted me to be. Whatever his reasons, I was out of it for weeks. I couldn't eat, barely slept, and became a shadow of myself. It was, and still is, the worst thing anyone has ever

25

bat in position on my shoulder. Abject terror—were they going to rape and murder me? All-out panic—oh God, how could I defend myself, a lone woman, against two grown men? Steely resolve—if they planned to hurt me, I was taking at least one of them down with me.

Thank God their intrusion had tripped the burglar alarm system, and the private security response team arrived quickly. But those ten minutes of terror and powerlessness robbed me of my appetite for countless days afterward and stole my peace for years to come.

In one heart-stopping second, my beloved refuge became my prison, and I never slept peacefully in that house again. It looked beautiful on the outside, but insecurity and fear ruled on the inside.

The luxury car was no better. I'd bought it because I'd let my partner convince me that it was the kind of car a vice president of a major corporation should drive. The car was beautiful, and it sure was fast, but it became a nightmare to maintain. Every time something broke—especially the low-profile rims that kept cracking because of the potholes that riddled the road up the hill to the beautiful, broken-into house—it cost me an arm, two legs, and half a lung to repair. Anxiety rode shotgun every time I drove that beautiful, broken car.

This, then, was the morass of my great-looking life: the hated job, the toxic relationship, and the burdensome possessions. I didn't want to let go of any of it, so I didn't let myself think too deeply about my situation. Instead, I told myself to keep doing what was necessary to make a good life for myself and my partner. Still, in the back of my mind, the ghosts of my childhood memories called to me— memories of feeling special to God and believing He had exceptional plans for me. They were faint and seemed too wispy to break me out of the grip of the things trapping me in a life I no longer wanted.

Thank goodness that wispy was strong enough for God to work with.

3

THE SLIDE TO ROCK BOTTOM

But God will redeem my soul from the power of the grave, for He shall receive me. Selah. Psalm 49:15 NKJV

For years, I sank deeper into unhappiness in my great-looking life. For years, I silently begged God to fix my life so I'd be happy. And for years, I almost buckled under the weight of what seemed like His divine silence. Not only did I stop believing I was special to God, but I was convinced He didn't love me and I didn't matter to Him.

Can you blame me? I was drowning in misery and begging Him to save me with no result that I could see. Once, I literally fell to my knees in my kitchen, weeping out of my distress and pleading with Him to help me. Can you guess what I got in return? That's right—crickets. It felt like God hadn't answered my prayers in *forever,* which left me feeling rejected and unloved by Him, and that broke my heart to pieces.

Besides my deep unhappiness in every area of my life, my belief that God didn't love me was my most closely guarded

31

secret. I was so terrified to admit it that I even held it back from my prayer journal. I felt unrighteous and sort of unsettled, even thinking that God didn't love me because I was afraid He would smite me and send me directly to hell. Since I was a pro at pretending, you can probably guess what I did. Yup, I pretended like I believed God loved me.

During that miserable time, I hardly ever missed church on Sunday. I wept through just about every praise and worship session, looking like I was backstroking through my blessings, but I was drowning in despair. If you'd asked me why I was crying, I couldn't have expressed my emotions because I didn't understand what I was feeling. All I knew was, those crying sessions helped reset my emotional pressure valve so I could make it through one more week without falling apart.

I know now that some were tears of sorrow over decisions that had taken me lightyears off track from the life I'd dreamed of living. Others were tears of despair that I'd never get back on track. Some were tears of frustration because my life had no joy and meaning in the way I knew it should, and I didn't know how to create those feelings. And the rest of my tears? Well, they were tears flowing straight from my broken, rejected heart.

You see, I wasn't a member of the church I attended—the same one where I wept through praise and worship every Sunday—but I'd tried to be. A few years before, I'd applied for membership, but they rejected my application.

I'd been a regular in those pews for several years, volunteered in a couple of ministries, and donated to various ongoing funds. I believed in this church's mission and ministry and in Jesus Christ's death, burial, and resurrection. Plus, I was a baptized Christian—not through this church, but still—and I read my Bible almost every day. As far as I was concerned, I was a shoo-in for membership. So you can imagine my shock when, sitting in the membership pastor's office, thinking he'd asked to meet with me as a mere formality, I heard him say, "We can't accept your application." To this day, I can still see the compassion on his face as he said it from across the expanse of his desk. Meanwhile, I sat stupefied for long seconds before finding my voice.

"But why?" I just managed to croak around the lump forming in my rapidly closing throat. The unexpected rejection cut deep, but I needed to know.

He told me that it came down to one reason: I was living with a man to whom I wasn't married, and the church wouldn't accept me until I remedied the situation. The meeting ended quickly after that. He'd said what he needed to say, and I was hanging on to my composure by a thread. I needed to get out of there before I broke down completely. And a breakdown was coming for sure, I could tell.

I felt filthy and unworthy as I hurried away from his office, my eyes glued to my feet. These good people—even in my pain, I still knew they were good people—had judged me, and I'd fallen short. I could almost feel the scarlet letter forming on my chest. I speed-walked across the church parking lot with tears burning the back of my eyes, too embarrassed to make eye contact with anyone. Moments later, as I sat in my car, I finally let the searing pain lance through me. My body heaved with gasping sobs, my head resting on the steering wheel, as rejection, shame, and heartbreak darn near suffocated me.

I thought God had said I should come to Him as I was. They—His body, His church—had said so as they invited me to join them. But when I came, they said I wasn't good enough. They said I needed to clean myself up before I was acceptable. With this rejection coming on top of my mountain of unanswered prayers, it's no wonder I was unsure if God loved me.

Still, as rejected as I felt, I kept returning to that church Sunday after Sunday because, somewhere deep down in an unacknowledged part of me, I knew they were right. Unlike anyone else in my life up to that point, they loved me enough to tell me, in their own clumsy way, that the life I had chosen was far out of step with God's will or His best for me. I also kept going to church and seeking God because, as much as I doubted His love, I was desperate for soul-saving hope that maybe—just maybe, despite everything—He actually did love me after all and would save me from my misery and unfulfillment. Plus, what else was I going to do? Nothing else had worked, and I was fresh out of options.

Now, years on the other side of that misery-soaked season in my life, I ache for the woman I was then: a woman whose pain, self-doubt, and hidden desperation saturated the pages of her prayer journals. I didn't share the full extent of my misery with anyone because I couldn't trust anyone— including my partner—with the potentially life-destroying truth hiding behind my mask. So I suffered in silence.

On the outside, I worked hard to maintain the life I'd built, hoping it would all come right eventually. In the privacy of my early-morning quiet times, I hunted through my Bible for a silver bullet to miraculously solve all my problems. Meanwhile, I teetered on the edge of hopelessness that God would ever get with it and *help me already!* Little did I know, He was about to show up in the most unexpected ways.

THE DESCENT BEGINS

Looking back, I'm sure God was waiting for me to hit rock bottom. In His divine wisdom, He knew that only then would I take His hand of rescue, escape the trap of a life I'd built, and run towards the dreams He planted in me without looking back.

My slide to rock bottom started with rumors of redundancy. The company decided it was a good time to restructure, and it planned to use the opportunity to ditch some dead weight. Through the corporate grapevine, I heard whispers of my name being on the list of the axed. Once the initial shock wore off, I wasn't surprised. Sure, I'd been trying to hide my growing dissatisfaction with my job, but it must have leaked out of me all over the place anyway. Plus, even though I was running a whole division of the company that I'd successfully set up from scratch, I guess my boss finally realized I was never going to be a good fit for his cutthroat team culture. I was the weakest link and it was time to get rid of me.

Still, when I heard the rumors, it hurt. In previous roles, I was the one making others redundant, and I never once thought I'd be on the other side of the desk.

Oh, did it hurt! It hurt to think I was no longer useful, necessary, or valuable. It hurt because my work and position were integral to my identity. And it hurt because it felt like the company was labeling me as no longer good enough and rejecting me.

Even as I fought through my feelings, I got practical. I set my finances in order so I could cover my mortgage, car payments, and life in general for the time I would be out of work, which I hoped wouldn't be more than a few months. I made a list of what I wanted to demand in my redundancy package so I'd be ready when the call came. I also started looking for jobs and slowly clearing my personal items out of my office.

While I waited for the axe to fall, I alternated between fear ("What will I do for work now? Who will hire me after redundancy?") and relief ("No more daily struggle going to a job I hate. Woohoo!"). Deep down, I *knew* this was God at work because, for the previous two years, He'd been prompting me to leave that job. Standing at my office window all those countless times, I knew He wanted me to step out of that job. Yet, even knowing this, I'd clung to the dead season because I was afraid to let go of it.

I mean, why would I willingly let it go? God was asking me to release one thing without giving me something else to hold on to. He gave me no answers about what to do with my life instead, no hint about the direction He wanted me to go in, and no roadmap to get there. Let me tell you, I wasn't game for *any* of that. So I clung to the job I dreaded until one morning in mid-2014 when my boss called me to his office. I knew this was it. In less than five minutes, with my ex-boss not once looking me in the eye and without even the clichéd, "Thanks for your years of hard work," my corporate career was over.

From the outside, it looked like the company turned me loose, but in truth, God used them as the first step in His mission to rescue me from my safe, self-made prison of an unfulfilling life. He had other plans for me, and as long as I kept clinging to what felt safe, those plans had zero prayer of unfolding. So He pried my first idol out of my hands. This was how, after sixteen years in the corporate world, with my walking papers in hand, I slunk home with my identity and self-worth in tatters.

I was out of a job and had no clue what to do next. I thought things couldn't get worse, but little did I know, my slide to rock bottom had only just begun.

THE GIRL I USED TO BE

When the daily trod to my hated corporate job ended, I dove into helping my partner in his business full-time. He thought and talked about work twenty-four seven, so I toiled twenty-four seven, all unpaid. It was awful, and I detested every minute because nothing I did was good enough. Until then, I'd felt like a failure as his woman. Now, on the heels of my job—a huge part of my identity—rejecting me, I also felt like a failure as a worker. I could hardly stomach my feelings of inadequacy and worthlessness, but, as was my habit, I choked them down, pretended everything was fine, and powered through. Meanwhile, my angst over our relationship kicked into high gear.

Early on, I had accepted that we would probably never get married, seeing as how, by his account, his previous experience with this institution was fairly harrowing. I see now that I sold myself short and lowered my standards while telling myself I was being practical.

By autumn 2014, the relationship felt like steel wool on an open sore. Still, I kept hitting up every available resource—self-help books, online courses, my willpower—to try transforming myself into the partner he wanted and believed he deserved. Eventually, I broke down and shared some of my doubts over my unhappy home life with a friend. She listened and then simply asked me, "Kris, how do you know that God doesn't have someone better for you?"

Her question stunned me into silence. In retrospect, planting that idea in my mind was the second step in God's rescue mission. I'd never once considered the possibility but now it tantalized me. Still, I clung to the relationship. I know, I know! But I'd sunk nearly a decade of my life—plus my heart, body, sense of self, and peace of mind—into it. Then he asked me to marry him. My shocked "Yes!" was a giant leap toward rock bottom.

I don't know how long he'd been thinking about proposing, but it seemed spontaneous on his part. There was no candlelight dinner, no flowers, and no engagement ring. I simply turned around from putting away some clothes in a dresser in our bedroom one Saturday afternoon to find him down on one knee. It was memorable in that I was a hot mess from my hair to my housedress—*so* not how any woman wants to be proposed to.

Looking back now, it seems odd that he asked me—the psychopathic attention whore—to marry him. Still, if you'd been present in that bedroom as he proposed, you'd have thought I was over the moon about it. I sure looked ecstatic over what I thought was an impossible dream coming true. But, in truth, I was frantically trying to ignore my self-forged chains tightening around me.

Despite my misgivings, I jumped into wedding planning mode. I organized my bridal party, booked a location, contracted a local designer to design and make my dress, ordered the invitations, and started buying the wedding favors.

Everything went like clockwork until one night, just before Christmas 2014, a couple of months before the wedding. Here's what happened: he behaved in a way I didn't like while we were out with some of his family, but I said nothing. He called me out on the eye-roll I didn't quite manage to hide. I said he was acting like a horse's hiney (but I used a stronger word), and even though I said it so only he would hear, he erupted like Mt. Vesuvius. Over the next few days, he threw ten years of perceived sins in my face and made it clear that he wouldn't keep waiting for me to get my act together and become the woman he'd been telling me all along I should be.

I was so desperate to hang on to the relationship and so conditioned to take the blame for everything that went wrong in it that I degraded myself trying to get back in his good graces. At one point, I knelt at his feet and *begged* him to forgive me—this was how low I'd sunk, literally and emotionally.

Lucky for me, the more I begged, the more his heart hardened, and the harder his heart became, the more I secretly asked myself if this was the future I wanted. In retrospect, I can see that this was the third step in God's rescue mission. Still, over the next few days, I prayed like the world was coming to an end—which I guess it kind of was for me—and I clung to the disintegrating tatters of our relationship, hoping we'd sort ourselves out in our premarital counseling session that was scheduled for after the new year.

Four days before Christmas, God's fourth step came through an old high school friend. Sitting at her kitchen table, I broke down and spilled everything to her—my unhappiness in the relationship, this latest upset, and my agony over how to fix my broken, misery-soaked life.

Once she let me get it all out, she looked me dead in the eye and said, "This isn't the Kris I knew from high school. That girl was bold and fearless." Her words were like a backhand to my face and a stab to my belly all at once. But they also ripped the scales off my eyes, reminded me of the brave, confident girl I used to be, and exposed the shadow I'd become.

As I looked at myself in the mirror that night just before bed, her words echoed in my heart, and I didn't like who I saw looking back at me. Not one little bit. I wanted to be that bold, fearless girl again, which put me exactly where God wanted me.

Less than an hour after my self-loathing session in front of the bathroom mirror, my partner—having started another midnight conversation accusing me of not doing anything to fix the problems I'd caused—hurled, "Maybe we should break up!" at me. This turned out to be the fifth step in God's rescue mission.

As I opened my mouth for the next round of begging for another chance to be a better woman for him, the Holy Spirit spoke to me audibly for the first time in my life. He said, "Kris, this is the last chance I'm giving you. Take it and run." So I did. I gently lobbed back at my partner, "You're right, we should break up." With those words, I started the climb back up from rock bottom without once looking back.

4

THE PEACE OF GOD (AND A WHOLE LOT MORE)

And the peace of God, which surpasses all understanding,
will guard your hearts and your minds in Christ Jesus.
Philippians 4:7 ESV

My main emotion when the relationship ended was relief at my sudden freedom. Plus shock, since I hadn't seen the end coming. And peace. Glorious peace.

I had no job and I'd just flushed ten years of my life down the toilet. But I was giddy and at peace because I now knew firsthand God's rescuing grace and limitless love for me.

Over the years, I'd stopped believing God loved me, that I was special to Him, and that He had extraordinary plans for my life. But when I finally allowed Him to pry my toxic relationship out of my stubbornly grasping fingers, I finally understood the truth: He loves me so much that He'll rescue me from a situation in which I haven't lifted a finger to rescue myself. That one fact showed me the truth: God *never* ignores me and *always* has my back, even when I don't.

Still, within hours of that final break, my mind shifted to practical matters. One big consideration was the house. I was eager to sever every tie between my new ex-partner and me, and the house was a big one, so it needed to be sold quickly. This was why, on the last day of 2014, I had my real estate agent list the house. My original plan was to keep living there until it sold, and my ex-partner planned to do the same. However, within two days, I reversed my decision.

The night I went to bed with my bedroom door locked and my taser in my hand because I felt threatened by his erratic behavior was the night I decided that I didn't want a *War of the Roses* situation for myself. I knew it was time to go. That very night, I messaged my parents to let them know I'd be moving out that weekend and asked if I could stay with them. I also asked my mom to come and stay with me for the next day and night. I needed a buffer that I could trust between my ex-partner and me. Plus, I needed her to help me pack up all my stuff to move.

Come the first Saturday of 2015, I said sayonara to my home of just under seven years and moved into my parents' guest room. I put my furniture and most of my belongings into storage and hunkered down to figure out my life.

By the time the moving truck drove away from my parents' house that afternoon, my emotional high had worn off. I knew my parents were happy to have me, and they told me how ecstatic they were that I was out of the relationship. Still, I was embarrassed and a little depressed that this was what I had come to. I mean, who loses their job, their relationship, and their house and moves into their parents' guest room at almost thirty-nine years old, all within six months? No one that I knew, that was for sure. So, as you can imagine, I felt like an epic failure.

Of course, the accursed car had to go too. As much as it felt like I was piling another failure on top of my already towering pile of failures, I had to be practical. After all, I was unemployed. What use did I have for a problem-plagued luxury car for which I was still paying from my savings? However, getting the car back from my ex-partner—who had driven off in it just before the moving truck had arrived to help me liberate myself from our ex-house—brought its own drama. Whatever his reasons, he seemed to feel that he needed my car more than I did, and he dismissed me each time I asked him for it.

The day he drove past me comfortably posed up in my beautiful Mercedes Benz while I steered my mom's old Toyota Rav4 in the other direction was the day I lost it. The old me would have kept begging him for my car, but I was tired of feeling like his victim, so I decided it was time to take my power back. I promptly got a lawyer, who got the police involved. I got my car back faster than you can say, "Jail time, buddy!"

The day after he returned the car to me, I sent it off to a used car lot to have it sold. And with that, almost every idol and treasure hoard I'd been clinging to—the job, relationship, house, and car—melted away like so much butter under a flaming desert sun.

At that point, I thought I'd lost, released or given away everything I had to lose, release, or give away. But God had two more things He needed me to get rid of before He could get to work on me.

STRIPPED BARE

Seeing as how I no longer had a house—or a job to help pay for one—for the next twelve months, I lived in my mom's guest room, my sister's guest room, and a friend's guest room. I also drove my mom's car, my sister's car, and my friend's car when I needed to move around. Meanwhile, I almost completely withdrew from any type of social life because I didn't want to be around most of the people I knew.

First, there were my former colleagues. With my redundancy, most of them started treating me like a pariah; a few even acted like they didn't know me. Besides feeling rejected by them, I was also embarrassed because of my loss of status. Plus, I didn't want to face their judgment and pity over my diminished circumstances.

Then there were the people I realized meant me no good and only wanted to get the dirt on my failed life. They would call, presumably to check up on me, but we were never long into the conversation before they started angling for the inside scoop on what had gone down in my relationship.

Except for a handful of people who showed themselves to genuinely care about me, I withdrew from them all. I deleted their numbers from my phone, unfollowed them on social media, and waited out the time until I became yesterday's news and they no longer cared about my story.

Besides getting rid of these relationships, I also sorted through what I had in storage and donated most of it. I was no longer the person who had bought them, and I didn't want most of it anymore, so I spared nothing; not the furniture, household items, clothes, shoes, or handbags.

By the time 2015 was over, I was stripped bare of everything that society had told me I should acquire or accomplish if I wanted to be successful. My corporate career was over, my long-term relationship, house, car, and possessions were gone, and I didn't even need all ten of my fingers to count the friends I had left.

On the surface, my life had gone down in a flaming ball of failure. But underneath, I was reaping the harvest of years of anguished cries for God's rescue. He'd heard every prayer I thought had fallen on His deaf ears, and now He answered every one of them, but not in the way I was looking for. I expected Him to wave His divine wand and make everything good again, to magically make me happy in the circumstances I wanted for myself. Instead, He stripped off all my masks, destroyed all my idols, and rid me of my treasure hoards. He put me in the perfect position to start afresh.

THE GIFT OF SALVATION

I was baptized when I was thirteen years old, but in early 2015, I was truly born again. In the wake of the wreckage left by my plummet to rock bottom, I committed my life to God—for real this time—and started my true spiritual education.

As a pastor's kid, I grew up in church where I let myself be spoon-fed with clichéd half-truths and watered-down religious doctrines. Plus, in the time leading up to my fall from grace, I'd practically lived in my Bible, looking for how I could get God to solve my problems and take away my misery. The one thing I hadn't done was explore the Word to discover how I fit into His story.

Now, I was hungry to know God intimately. I devoured His Word, voraciously listened to Joyce Meyer's practical teachings, read books to uplift my spirit, fasted, and sank into prayer, keeping up running conversations with God throughout each day.

You see, when you hit this kind of low point in your life, you finally understand salvation—Jesus's sacrificial deliverance from your sins and His securing of your place in the Father's eternal kingdom. Gratitude for His saving love overwhelms you, especially when you know you couldn't do a darn thing to save yourself.

All along, you think God isn't listening to your desperate pleas. But when you hit rock bottom, you realize He was always in the wings, waiting for you to let go of your idols and take hold of His gift of salvation, which He never forces on you.

God waited until I was ready to leave the abusive relationship behind with zero regrets so I wouldn't be like Lot's wife and look back. He waited until I was over the highfalutin job so I wouldn't chase after another one on the world's say-so. He waited until I released my death grip on my possessions so I wouldn't clutter up my life and edge Him out again. And He waited until His opinion mattered more to me than other people's.

The moment I embraced His gift of salvation for real, I stopped trying to fill the hole in my heart with people's approval and the world's version of success, and I let Him slip right into that space instead. And do you know what? He fit perfectly.

WHO ARE YOU?

My road to freedom started with me accepting God's hand of rescue and His gift of salvation, and allowing Him to strip me of all my idols. It continued with a punch to the gut from a question a friend asked me in her living room. When she asked me the question, I stared at her in shock for a few seconds before my face crumpled. I sobbed as I doubled over on her living room floor, my body heaving as I struggled to get myself under control.

"Who are you, Kris?"

This question had me collapsing in shock and tears, scared and confused because I didn't have a clue. It would be two years before I could finally answer her question. But really, how could I have known then who I was? I was fresh out of a ten-year relationship with a man who didn't believe in God. Plus, I spent my entire adult life to that point chasing what the world told me I should want: an important job, a beautiful house, a fancy car, the latest trends, and money in the bank. In the process of pursuing these things, I'd lost myself. Of course I had! God never intended for me to travel that path, so of course, I ended up wandering away from who He made me to be. No wonder I was an untethered, lost mess by the time I was made redundant from the hifalutin, dread-inducing job, broke up with the agnostic, abusive boyfriend, sold the trouble-riddled house and car, and gave away all my possessions.

What answer could I possibly have given when my friend asked, "Who are you, Kris?" Ex-executive? Ex-live-in girlfriend? Ex-owner of a bunch of cool stuff? I had tied my identity to my accomplishments and position, so of course, I was anchorless and adrift without them. Worse yet, I had no idea how to find my way back to me.

But oh, how gracious our God is! He does some of His best work when you're at your worst. When you've lost track of yourself, He can lead you back to who you are meant to be *through Him*. This was how I found my *true* identity this time: through God's Word. It's in His Word that, little by little, you start to learn about who He is and how He feels about you. Then, when you get a revelation—not head knowledge but truly knowing in your heart—about the depth and breadth of His love for you, you start seeing yourself in and through Him.

My friend never again asked me, "Who are you, Kris?" Still, about two years after she did, it suddenly dawned on me one day that God's Word had given me the answer. I'm the good Father's daughter, created in His image, saved by His grace, and made to do good works. I'm a woman overcome by God's mercy and love, trying to pay it forward because it's the only way I know to show how grateful I am to Him. I'm a servant, dead set on fulfilling my Master's call on my life because I want to hear, "Well done, good and faithful Kris," when the time comes. I'm Jesus' sister and friend, who's constantly filled with and fed by the Holy Spirit. And, above all, I'm God's precious love.

It took me two years to get to that point and, thank God, by His grace, I'm still discovering who He made me to be.

5

HITTING RESET

*But—When God our Savior revealed his kindness and love,
he saved us, not because of the righteous things we had
done, but because of his mercy. He washed away our sins,
giving us a new birth and new life through the Holy Spirit.*
Titus 3:4-5 NLT

There I was, hanging out in my parents' guest room, feeling all the feels. I was elated by my brand-new freedom and blissed out from my recommitment to God. But I was also clueless about who I was, mortified over my epic backward leap in life, and panicked over what the heck to do with my future.

As a natural planner, I was *so* not okay with feeling adrift. I was okay with being directionless and unproductive for a time, but not knowing how long that time would last straight-up terrified me. I needed to fix the problem *now* so I could escape the discomfort of uncertainty.

As I sorted the things and people out of my life, I hunkered down to chart a new path to joy and fulfillment. Unfortunately, I didn't have the first clue where to start, which shot my panic into the stratosphere. Then my friend who had asked me, "What if God has someone better for you?" reminded me that I didn't need to rush. She pointed out that what I was looking at as unproductive and directionless was God giving me the gift of space and time to wait on Him for my next step. After fasting and praying, I came to the same conclusion, and my anxiety eased.

Once I stopped panicking, I realized that obligations to a job, a particular career path, a partner, or a chosen lifestyle no longer constrained me. It dawned on me that this was too good an opportunity to waste. It was my golden opportunity to hit the reset button on my life, to make new, radically different decisions, and to go after God's plan for me with a single-minded focus and zero concern about anyone else's opinions.

After chasing the world's plan for decades, I was confident that God's plan would be incomparably better. I had only one problem: how on earth was I supposed to discover His plan?

THE RESURRECTION OF THE DEAD

I asked God for a burning bush once. I was eighteen years old and about to enter university, and I needed clear, undisputable instructions from Him on what to do with my life. This decision would influence my life for years to come, so I wanted specifics, including a big vision and a complete roadmap for how to get there.

I went to God in prayer, asked what He wanted me to do, and waited for Him to drop the answer into my spirit. I didn't feel a thing, so I prayed again and waited for a sign. Still nothing, so I kept praying and waiting, praying and waiting.

Eventually, my frustration and impatience boiled over. I was on a schedule with a deadline for deciding, so I threw a spiritual tantrum and demanded a burning bush moment from God. Other than an angelic visitation, you can't get clearer than that, right?

But God was unmoved by my demands, so I got mad at Him and decided I was in charge of my life from here on out. That decision was the worst one of my life because it led me away from God and into years of heartache. That decision caused me to choose the world's vision, the world's definition of success, and the world's way of operating over what He wanted of me and what He had for me. That one decision led me to abandon God's standards for me, and it caused me to lose my identity.

So, as I set about figuring out how to put my imploded life back together, I knew I wanted to walk in God's plan for me and not go astray again. But where to start? Over the years, whenever my desperation and misery surged to uncontrolled levels, I had done all the things that promised to reveal my purpose: I took career tests and personality quizzes, read books about finding my calling and even considered going back to university for a whole new degree.

Once, I even endured what felt like the most useless Christian career counseling session in the history of the world. All I wanted was to know how to find God's calling for me, but all the counselor would give me was, "God's calling for your life is to serve Him." I almost rolled my eyes clear out of my head when he said it, but I managed to catch myself and keep my face neutral. I mean, what was I supposed to do with his useless cookie-cutter response? I needed actionable advice! So I tried again, but he skillfully sidestepped my question, sticking to his script and droning on with his empty-sounding spiritual pep talk.

Over the years, nothing I'd tried had worked—not the quizzes, counseling, friendly advice, or books. So, sitting in my parents' guest room, you can imagine how lost I felt about where to turn now that I was working with a clean slate. Ironically, this put me in the perfect state of mind to find the answer I needed.

I stumbled across a find-your-purpose article that recommended thinking back to my earliest childhood desire of what I wanted to do when I grew up. Shockingly, where all else had failed, this worked! The wisp of an old dream floated into my mind. I ruminated on it for a while, but no matter how I came at it, I always circled back to this same desire—every single time.

Eventually, the truth dawned on me: God had planted this desire in my heart *from the very beginning* as the tiny seed that would grow into His purpose for my life. My job had

56

been to water and nurture it to full bloom. Instead, I'd let the world scoff at my dream and convince me it was stupid. Plus, I'd bought the lie that going after my dream was supposed to be easy, feel good, and happen quickly and in one miraculous leap. But every time I'd tried to nurture that little kernel of a dream, I'd met stumbling blocks, roadblocks, and mental blocks. Eventually, I became disillusioned and turned my back on the precious seed God had planted in me, hoping it would wither away and die. Thank God, it never did.

As I remembered my dried-up, mostly dead seed of a dream, I allowed God to fan the flame of my desire to pursue it into a roaring fire. Then, I took my first step to go after it. I bought a plane ticket.

A SILLY, FRIVOLOUS DREAM

Being a tourist is nice, but I always wanted travel to be a big part of how I define myself and live my life. I wanted to reside in foreign countries and explore places that were far off the beaten-to-death, overly Instagramed paths that most others love to trample.

Back in high school, I dreamed of being a U.N. translator because it was the only career I knew of that could open up the world to me. But I didn't like studying Spanish, so I abandoned the dream. Then, in my middle teens, I got hooked on *National Geographic* magazines. I loved disappearing into other parts of the globe through its pages, hoping one day I'd figure out a career that would take me to those places.

When I left university with my actuarial degree in hand, I decided to give my real dream one last shot. I went after jobs with diplomatic missions, airlines, and even travel agencies. I tested every door I knew of to get a foot into the world of travel, but every door slammed shut on my foot. Eventually, I accepted that the world was right and my dream was stupid. After all, how could wanderlust be anyone's God-given dream? Who could I help by living like a nomad most of the time? Besides, if it was meant for me, it shouldn't be this hard. So I gave up, landed my first corporate job, and followed the world's plan to misery and dissatisfaction.

But now, as I started grappling my way up from rock bottom, I decided to believe that my beautiful, neglected, God-given dream *wasn't* stupid, trivial, or far-fetched. More importantly, I finally understood that—as frivolous as it looked to the world—God had given this dream to me as a first step on the path He'd laid out for my life. Seeing as, after years of shame and neglect, I hadn't managed to extinguish its flame, He must still have a way to use my dream—and me—to build His kingdom. So I fired up my laptop and prepared to storm the travel world.

A GOD-GIVEN, LIFE-CHANGING DREAM

Having resurrected my mostly dead God-given dream of travel, I decided to pursue it. But when I remembered the last two years of my corporate life—staring out my office window, wondering what all my hard work was for—I knew I had to help people as I reinvented myself and my life. Otherwise, I'd end up right back in a place of dissatisfaction, feeling stuck and unfulfilled. The field of international development checked all my boxes, so I got to work trying to find a job. And trying, and trying, and trying.

Here's the thing: just because you decide to follow God's plan doesn't mean the rest of the world will hop on and ride the purpose train with you to success and glory. Doors won't magically open in the blink of an eye, supporters won't pop out of the woodwork the next day, and the stars won't miraculously align to make all your dreams come true in one glorious, breath-stealing moment.

Going in, I didn't know that international development is locked up tighter than Fort Knox against anyone who hasn't built their career in it from the ground up. I didn't know that my management skills and almost two decades of corporate experience meant less than nothing to them. Still, I kept at it.

Countless applications and six disheartening months of rejections later, I finally landed a volunteer position with a small foreign non-governmental organization in Indonesia. It wasn't the high-powered international change-making role I imagined for myself, but it was exactly what God knew I needed, and I couldn't pack my suitcase fast enough.

Still, before I kicked off my life-transforming season as an international volunteer, God sent me on adventures that would start healing my broken heart and soul. He started showing me what true freedom looked, tasted, and felt like.

6

GET UP AND GO

But don't just listen to God's word. You must do what it says. Otherwise, you are only fooling yourselves. James 1:22 NLT

For years, I had talked about the places I wanted to visit, but in all that time, I never did anything to actually visit them. In the spring of 2015, while I was still trying to figure out my job situation, I decided the time for talking was over, and the time for doing had come.

For my first journey, my sister and I headed to Cuba for a week. Visiting Jamaica's nearest neighbor had been on my bucket list for years, but I'd dismissed my desire to go there, mainly because my ex-partner wasn't interested. Now, since I was no longer making decisions based on other people's opinions, off I went with my sister.

It was wonderful and felt like freedom. We barely did anything for five days and hardly left the resort where we'd booked in, but I didn't care. All that mattered was that I was someplace I'd never been before—someplace I'd always wanted to go. Those five days fed my soul.

At the end of our time in Cuba, we returned home to Jamaica, and I went back to trying to figure out my next step.

With no job yet on the horizon and no one holding me back, I decided to accept a friend's invitation to visit her in Tanzania. With that one decision, God set me on an unexpected, accelerated path to healing.

But more on that shortly.

As I started planning my trip, I decided to stay in Tanzania for a month. Because of flight routings, I added short stops in Amsterdam and Istanbul to my itinerary. Then I started thinking bigger. Why not see Alaska while I was at it? I'd dreamed of going there for years, but no one I knew was interested in cold places, so I'd let them pooh-pooh my desire to visit this mysterious, beautiful place. Since I no longer care about others' approval, I added an Alaskan cruise to my plan.

Then, another friend invited me to visit her in Canada while I was at it. I added visiting an aunt in New York to my itinerary to round things out.

One by one, I applied for the visas I needed for what I dubbed my Epic Trip of 2015. Meanwhile, I started booking everything—flights, airport transfers, hotels, and the cruise and shore excursions. I stopped talking about all the places I wanted to see and the things I wanted to do, and I got busy setting myself up to see places and do things. And wouldn't you know it? When I stepped out and started doing and seeing things related to my tiny, resurrected dream, God began to heal my heart, mind, and body.

FALLING IN LOVE

I first got on a plane as a small child, but I set off on the first big journey of my life in mid-2015. Anticipation zinged through my body as I waited to board my first flight at the airport in Kingston, Jamaica. I knew what I had planned but didn't truly know what was ahead of me. Even so, as wired as I was, it felt like the whole airport should have known that I was setting off on a momentous journey. On paper, I was heading to Europe, Africa, and North America, but in reality, God was showing me what was possible when I honored the vision He'd given me.

My first stop was Amsterdam, where I arrived early on a Sunday morning near the end of June 2015. I checked into my hotel, dropped off my bags, and headed back out the door to pack in as much as possible before jetlag from my sleepless nine-hour flight hit me. I spent the day steeped in European history and culture in the Museumplein, marveled over Dutch engineering and water management as I boated around some of the city's canals, sampled Dutch pancakes, and developed my first crush on a country.

The next day, I headed into the Dutch countryside, and my crush transformed into real love. The scenery was stunning, with a beauty so sharp that it almost hurt my eyes. I couldn't keep the grin off my face all day, and I didn't care if I looked like a simpleton. I was too delighted to be walking around in my impossible, resurrected dream to care. I saw working windmills, quaint villages that I thought only existed in Hallmark movies, a cheese factory, authentic wooden shoes, Delft blue pottery, and The Hague, which had existed for me only in news reports.

By the end of my two jam-packed days in Amsterdam, I was lounging on cloud nine, pleasantly tired and flushed with love. My heart was bursting with light and pleasure instead of misery and darkness for the first time in literal years. I didn't know it then, but this unlikely love started to heal me.

In truth, my Epic Trip wasn't helping anyone but me. But looking back now, I understand that before God could use me in service to others, He needed to start healing me from my broken years. He needed to start cleaning off the muck of the pigsty I'd been living in. He started with the Netherlands and, oh my, did He continue with Tanzania.

BREAKING OLD BOUNDARIES

I flew nine hours from Amsterdam to Dar es Salaam to begin my first-ever visit to the continent of Africa. I went with an open mind but didn't expect to leave Tanzania a month later with my broken heart put back together again.

In my first week, I explored Dar es Salaam, the capital city of Tanzania. I learned a few quickly forgotten words of

Swahili, saw real-life hijab for the first time, visited artisans' workshops, and waded in the Indian Ocean. I saw the poor and polluted side of the city, sampled strong Tanzanian coffee, and stood amidst the busyness of the central market.

My heart broke in Bagamoyo, a coastal town where slaves were held before transportation to Zanzibar for further shipment to mostly Arab and Asian countries. I was shocked to learn that slavery wasn't abolished in Tanzania until 1922, almost one hundred years after the English-speaking Caribbean did away with it. Slavery had always seemed historically distant to me, but I kept thinking, "My grandma was already a young woman when the last slaves here were finally set free."

Walking around Bagamoyo, it never occurred to me that I'd also recently been set free.

As I traveled to different parts of the country over the next few weeks, my consciousness of life outside the narrow, limited box of my existence started expanding. By the end of my month in Tanzania, I was a different person, and I knew I could never stuff myself back into my old box.

As God was using Tanzania to expand the boundaries of my life, He was using my hostess' gourmet cooking skills to nourish my body. I'd never eaten so consistently well in my entire life. She made things I'd only ever heard about on cooking shows—things I thought were only served in fancy restaurants, things that smelled and tasted like ambrosia. She made each meal a feast for the senses, and my narrow food existence went right out the window during the weeks I spent dining at her table. Her meals were well-planned, nutritionally balanced, and beautifully presented, all without her slaving away in the kitchen. Because of her, by the time my month in Tanzania was over, my skin was glowing, my face was completely blemish-free for the first time since I was a teenager, and I felt healthy from the inside out.

My four weeks in Tanzania expanded my mind beyond its previous borders, but my body was also nourished in a way that it had never been before. I threw out what I thought I knew about healthy eating and let myself be schooled in new possibilities. I couldn't have asked for more from Tanzania, but it had something more to offer me—something huge.

HEALING WONDERS

In the second week of July 2015, a little under two weeks after arriving in Tanzania, I left Dar es Salaam for the country's interior. I was going on a four-day safari.

I flew from Dar es Salaam to Kilimanjaro Airport, then was driven to Arusha, where I would spend the night. That thirty-mile drive is burned into my memory because it was when I got my first clear view of Mt. Kilimanjaro and first dreamed of summiting what I later learned is the highest point on the continent of Africa. I didn't know it yet, but I would make the same drive to Arusha again six months later as I went after my new dream.

My safari began the next morning when Dearson, my safari driver and guide, collected me in a safari van from my hotel. He and I spent the next four days together in that van. He was the perfect guide: a fount of information when I wanted it, a comfortably silent companion when I needed it, and he knew where all the cool animals hung out. This last point was critical since my safari wasn't during the migration season, which is when it's easy to see the Big Five—lions, buffaloes, rhinos, elephants, and cheetahs. Over the four days of my safari, Dearson ensured that I saw them all.

Our safari van was like the third member of our little group. While driving on regular paved roads, I sat in front with Dearson. But when we were in the parks looking for animals, he would open the top of the van so I could stand with my entire upper body outside the vehicle for an unobstructed 360-degree view.

You may be surprised to know that, until the moment we set off from my hotel in Arusha, I hadn't thought about what a safari would be like. I didn't set off from the hotel with ideas about what I wanted to see or where I wanted to go. I truly had zero expectations and was open to whatever experiences came.

Dearson informed me as we drove away from the hotel that our first destination was Tarangire National Park. Surprisingly—to me, at least—the sharp beauty of the landscape as we drove there immediately started working on my heart. By the time we arrived at the park, I was already filled with quiet joy, high-fiving myself that I'd decided to do this. My quiet joy exploded into straight-up ecstasy when, minutes into the park, we came across my first-ever herd of elephants in the wild. They seemed to come out of nowhere as we drove along a path. As they approached our position on the dirt track, Dearson shut off the safari van, and silence descended. I asked a question or two about elephants but didn't say much because I didn't want to startle them. They could, after all, crush our van—and us along with it—like a tin can. But inside, I was squealing and jumping around like a little kid whose biggest wish had just come true.

I grinned like a loon all day as we traversed the park, thrilled to bits at the sight of zebras, giraffes, wild boars, monkeys, and gazelles. Whenever we came across a herd of animals, we would stop. Dearson would shut off the van, and silence would descend again, save for the sounds of nature. I felt at peace and exhilarated all at once.

In the late afternoon, we left Tarangire and headed to Maramboi, where we enjoyed a feast and then bedded down for the night. Even now, I remember falling asleep with praise in my heart and a gigantic smile on my lips. I couldn't have dreamed of a better day and was on the verge of bursting into sparkles over all I'd experienced.

I was beyond grateful for this adventure. From the lone giraffe I'd seen grazing by the side of the road that morning on the way to Tarangire to the herd of zebras grazing by my back porch as the sun set over Maramboi to the sound of a wild boar snuffling around outside my cabin as I drifted off to sleep, the wonder of what I was witnessing almost overwhelmed me.

Can you believe it got even better the next day?

7

"I LOVE YOU"

For the Lord your God is living among you. He is a mighty
savior. He will take delight in you with gladness. With his
love, he will calm all your fears. He will rejoice over you
with joyful songs. Zephaniah 3:17 NLT

Day two of my safari changed my life. I met God out there.

Dearson and I rose, had breakfast, and got on the road early because we had a lot to cover that day. As he had done the morning before, he gave me a brief outline of our route and plan for the day. We were going to the Serengeti, which I'd only ever seen in *National Geographic* magazines.

As we drove towards our destination, I still hadn't wrapped my mind around where we were going. Even the idea of it didn't seem real. We drove for a couple of hours across flatlands before ascending the wall of the East African Rift wall. I felt like I was driving through a nature documentary, and my perpetual smile stretched even broader. How could this be my actual life?

This very type of experience was what I dreamed of and thought was impossible as a teenager poring over *National Geographic* magazines. Quiet tears slipped down my cheeks as we wound our way up the wall, and I absorbed the fact that I was literally driving through my dream. God bless Dearson—he'd been telling me about the Rift Valley but fell silent as he sensed the moment's weight.

Eventually, we arrived at the Ngorongoro Conservation Area and checked in at the gate before continuing our journey up the mountain. As we ascended, the weather turned foggy, chilly, and damp. The higher up we went into the fog and dampness, the more I felt like God was wrapping His arms around me. At one point, I felt the words, like a whisper in my heart, "Kristine, my daughter, I love you so very much."

I tried to be quiet, but tears cascaded down my cheeks as we kept ascending, and I felt His love and peace wrap me up like He would never let me go. My love of mountains was born then, in the first place and in the first moment when I felt God as a physical presence in my life.

UNBREAK ME

As we continued down the other side of the mountain, we passed Maasai villages and herds of animals. Then, suddenly, we were at the entrance to Serengeti National Park.

After checking in and devouring our packed lunches, Dearson and I set off into this new wilderness. Within minutes, we came upon a pride of lions lolling about in the shade of a tree, relaxing while the sun and heat were at their peak. My delight was immediate but paled compared to what I felt later that day. You see, God used the Serengeti to unbreak my heart.

I was standing with my head through the open roof of the safari van as we drove across the endless plains when the reality of where I was and what I was doing body-slammed me. The beauty of my surroundings pressed in on me, and I knew that if I wanted to fit it all into my heart, I had to let go of the darkness lingering there.

I was already working on forgiving the hurts I had toted around for the past several months, but that was the moment when I truly forgave it all: my ex-company for rejecting me, my ex-partner for how he treated me, my friends and family for not telling me what they saw and knew, my ex-colleagues for turning their backs on me, my ex-friends for not caring about me, and myself for my bad judgment and wrong decisions. I let go of even older hurts that I thought were long gone—old betrayals, offenses, and mistakes.

Bathed in the afternoon sun of the Serengeti, God brought all the darkness inside me out into the light, and I let it all go. How could I keep harboring dark ugliness in my heart as I stood in the awesome privilege of this experience? Out in the Serengeti, God used the stunning majesty of His creation as an invitation for me to lay it all down and let Him clean it all up. As I accepted His invitation, my heart began to heal.

A POSTCARD FROM GOD

I saw lions, elephants, gazelles, giraffes, and hyenas as we roamed the endless plains of the Serengeti that afternoon. The scenery was so sharp and clear that I felt like it must have been photoshopped.

"Dearson," I murmured at one point, "I feel like we're driving through God's postcard."

Since it was the dry season, our safari van kicked up a lot of dust. And because I spent most of that blissful afternoon hanging out the roof of the van, my hair was beyond a hot mess. But I did not care one whit. My awesome encounters with God were more than worth dusty, ugly hair.

As dusk crept in, we arrived at our resting place for the night—Kati Kati, a camp of tents in the heart of the Serengeti. I had a shower, ate dinner, and called it a night. After I poured out my thanks to God, I fell asleep to the sound of hyenas wailing somewhere out in the surrounding wilderness. At this point, I was happier than I'd ever hoped to be in my entire life. My dreams of joy back in the middle of my misery only a year before were laughably anemic compared to the reality of this experience. What's more, as I fell asleep on my comfortable cot in Kati Kati, I was a different woman from the one who had awoken fourteen hours earlier in Maramboi.

You don't come into the presence of God or lay down your burdens—much less do both in one day—and stay the same. For that alone, Tanzania secured a special place in my heart forever.

THE BIG FIVE

On day three of the safari, we had breakfast and bid farewell to Kati Kati just before dawn. After the previous day spent crossing Ngorongoro, crisscrossing a small part of the vast Serengeti, encountering the presence of God, and having my broken heart put back together again, I needed nothing else. We could have been done with the safari right then, but we still had two more days to go, and I was eager for any and everything God had for me out there.

The sun broke over the horizon as Dearson and I set off in our safari van. Minutes after leaving Kati Kati, we rounded a corner and almost collided with a huge herd of buffalo, about three hundred by Dearson's reckoning. Before we knew it, they had us surrounded, and in the background, behind a grove of acacia trees, a hot air balloon rose with the sun. The scene, forever etched into my brain and on my heart, couldn't have been more idyllic.

Later that morning, I saw my first herd of hippos, some ducks, and more hyenas and lions. After a bit of a chase,

Dearson even managed to get us close to two cheetahs. Then, around mid-morning, we left Serengeti, heading back to Ngorongoro. We had a collapsed volcano to explore.

Ngorongoro Crater is a caldera that formed when the mountain, an ex-volcano, collapsed in on itself. It's also home to a wide variety of wildlife, so we spent the afternoon driving around it, with me oohing and aahing over herds of zebras, elephants, gazelles, ostriches, and lions.

We ate our packed lunches overlooking a hippo-packed lake, and Dearson even managed to find a rhinoceros for me to gawk at through a pair of binoculars. With that sighting, he succeeded in making sure I saw Africa's Big Five with my own two eyes.

Late in the afternoon, we left the crater for Rhino Lodge, where we spent the last chilly, mountaintop night of my safari.

THE PRESENCE OF GOD

By the time we checked out at the Ngorongoro gate on the morning of day four of my safari, I felt like I'd lived a lifetime in the two days since we checked in there on our way to Serengeti. After everything I'd seen, how could I not?

We went back down the wall of the East African Rift, passing villages and towns along the way. Then back through Arusha to Kilimanjaro Airport, where my safari ended.

When I arrived back in Dar es Salaam that night, I didn't have words to explain to my hostess what those four days had done to me, but I think she understood. You can't encounter God the way you do on a safari—or when you're broken the way I was—and come back the same you were when you left. You can't come back with the same beliefs and perspectives you had when you set off. You surely can't come back believing there's no God.

If you go into the wilds of God's amazing creation with an open heart, you feel Him everywhere out there. Unlike our cities and in our everyday lives, when we easily forget His omnipresence, you can't escape God in the wilderness.

I didn't expect it, but those four days changed me. They freed me from the weight of my emotional baggage, drew me closer to God, showed me what intimacy with Him can be like, and made me fall in love with His creation. Now, I had one final must-do before I left Tanzania. It was time to visit Zanzibar.

A LESSON ON OFFENSE

Tanzania consists of the mainland plus the islands of Zanzibar, Pemba, and other islands in the Zanzibar Archipelago. My hostess decided to join me for this trip, so we took a puddle jumper from Dar es Salaam to Zanzibar.

Twenty minutes later, I landed smack-dab in the middle of my first experience of culture shock.

For the first time in my life, I saw real live women wearing burqas, and all I could think was, "How are they not passing out from heat stroke?" I wanted to gawk at them out of pure curiosity, but my society said staring is rude, so I restrained myself. However, this experience taught me a lesson that would help me in the years to come as I explored unfamiliar countries and cities: wanting to stare is a natural reaction when you're faced with the unusual or unfamiliar. In the far-flung places that I've visited since Zanzibar, *I'm* the unusual, unfamiliar thing at which people sometimes gawk. Instead of being offended, as I would have been before Zanzibar, I now understand their natural curiosity and barely notice anymore.

Back in Zanzibar, my host and I had a delicious lunch of octopus. Then I went off on a walking tour of Stone Town, visited the site of the old slave market, and took an afternoon jaunt by boat to Changuu Island to see endangered giant tortoises, one of which was over 150 years old. My mind boggled knowing that this tortoise was born before slavery was abolished in Tanzania.

The next day, I saw red colobus monkeys in Jozani Forest, explored a grove of mangrove trees, went on a short nature walk through a forest, visited a spice farm, and wrapped up the day over a rooftop dinner with my hostess.

The next morning, before we left the island, my hostess and I visited the Old Fort, where an unforgettable woman called Queenie painted both of my legs, one arm, and a shoulder with henna. I saw quite a bit on my quick two-day trip to Zanzibar, but that one hour in the Old Fort with the henna ladies was the most fun I had there.

That afternoon, we took another puddle jumper back to Dar es Salaam. A few days later, with my mind still blown and my heart still healing, I said goodbye to Tanzania.

8

HEALING, HEALING, AND MORE HEALING

O Lord, if you heal me, I will be truly healed; if you save me, I will be truly saved. My praises are for you alone!
Jeremiah 17:14 NLT

I left Tanzania on an emotional and spiritual high. I arrived there a broken wreck of a woman who was planning on having a great vacation and new adventures in a place that had never even been on my radar. I definitely had a great vacation and new adventures, but God gave me so much more! He gave me my heart back, He gave me my joy back, and He gave me a taste of true freedom. God used Tanzania to unbreak me and to begin healing me.

As I boarded my late-night flight at the airport in Dar es Salaam one month after I arrived there, I was grateful for it all, and the idea of returning to tackle Mt. Kilimanjaro was already taking root in my mind.

Kristine Bolt

LEARNING TO LISTEN AND OBEY

I flew from Dar es Salaam in Tanzania to Istanbul in Turkey, transiting through Amsterdam. This was where my luggage and I got separated for the first time. Back in those days, I suffered from luggage anxiety, with which I had struggled for years. You know that feeling, right? From the moment you check your bags at your departure airport until the moment you claim them off the carousel at your arrival airport, you suffer from low-level anxiety, wondering the whole time in the back of your mind if you and your bags will arrive together at your destination, on the same flight. I would even watch from my window seat as the baggage handlers loaded the plane's cargo hold, trying to catch a glimpse of my bags to be sure they got loaded.

All of this anxiety came not because I was super attached to my things but because I wasn't in control of them once they left my possession. Well, my fear finally came to pass. As I waited in Amsterdam to board my connecting flight to Turkey, I had a strong feeling that I should ask the gate agent to check that my bags had been transferred from my Dar es Salaam flight to my Istanbul flight. I dismissed the prompting.

"Don't be silly," I thought. "This is Schipol Airport, for goodness' sake. Of course your suitcases are on the plane!"

They weren't.

When we arrived in Istanbul almost three and a half hours later, my suitcases were very much still back in Amsterdam. I couldn't help it; I laughed, shook my head, and said, "Okay, Holy Spirit, lesson learned. When You tell me to do something, I'll do it. Good one, though!"

I would be in Istanbul for only two nights before departing for my next destination. This left the airline with very little wiggle room to fix the problem that my disobedience had caused. Still, I had a large tote with my clothes and toiletries for the next couple of days, so I hopped into a cab and headed for my hotel. Despite my luggage situation, I was determined to enjoy my very short time in a new city.

In my years of travel since my Schipol disobedience, I can declare without reservation or doubt that I've ditched anxiety over my checked luggage because God has worked on me about letting go of my need to keep a tight grip of control on everything. At least when it comes to my checked luggage, I've learned to use wisdom and let the rest go. Meanwhile, I've had to re-learn too many times to count the lesson of obeying the Holy Spirit's promptings and to stop trying to control everything.

ANOTHER NEW STANDARD

I spent my first afternoon in Istanbul wandering around the neighborhood where my hotel was located, buying a few small souvenirs, and reveling yet again in the reality of where I was. After dinner at a nearby restaurant, I returned to my gorgeous little boutique hotel near Topkapi Palace. That hotel was where I first appreciated an A-class bed and top-quality bedding. It felt like I was sinking into a cloud as I drifted off to sleep, and I don't think I moved an inch all night. I would surely have slept late the next morning if the first call to worship from a nearby mosque hadn't awoken me.

I'm sure kings and queens sleep on better beds than that one. But I'll remember it with fondness forever because it redefined and elevated my bedding standards, just as other experiences on my Epic Trip had been doing in other areas of my life. After the best night of sleep ever on The Bed That Changed Everything and a leisurely breakfast, I set off on a group tour to explore Istanbul's must-see spots. We visited Sultan Ahmet Square, Ayasofya, and a Turkish rug market where I had no intention of buying anything but broke down and bought a small rug. I couldn't help it! The rugs were absolutely gorgeous, and the quality was like nothing I'd ever felt in a rug. The moment I ran my hand over it, I envisioned my future home with the rug in front of the fireplace in my cozy living room. After having that vision, the salesman didn't need to work hard to get me to buy it.

As we boarded the tour bus a little while later, I asked myself what madness had caused me to buy a rug, for goodness sake, even a small one. I had no home or floor on which to lay it, and my luggage was already stuffed with purchases I'd made on my journey. I didn't have the space or circumstances for a whole rug! But I've never once regretted buying it.

You see, that small rug sparked the tiny ember of a new dream in me that would be fanned into a flame in the years to come. That one small rug started me off on creating a detailed vision of my new dream home, community, and life.

As I write this book, I'm still waiting for the vision to materialize. I have no doubt that it will because it was a promise from God straight to my heart.

After visiting the Grand Bazaar, we had lunch at the train station where the Orient Express used to end its service in Constantinople—Istanbul's previous name. As a huge Agatha Christie and Hercule Poirot fan, and since *Murder on the Orient Express* is one of my favorite mysteries, lunching at the Orient Express terminus had me ready to burst into sparkles all over again.

After lunch, we set off for the Blue Mosque, which was the first mosque I ever entered. Our visit to Ayasofya earlier that morning didn't count as visiting a mosque because it was still purely a museum and not a place of worship back then. That has since changed. We took our shoes off as we entered the Blue Mosque, and the women in our group covered our heads with the scarves we were told to bring. After a few minutes of walking around and learning a little about the mosque's history and importance, we left and wandered about in the nearby market, where I bought some Turkish delights to add to my luggage.

We ended the day with a tour of Topkapi Palace, which used to be the residence of the sultans of the Ottoman Empire. From there, I strolled down the street back to my hotel, where I enjoyed the quiet of its courtyard as evening crept across the city. The day had been long but good, and I hadn't thought about my missing luggage once.

Speaking of my luggage, it finally arrived late that night, only a few hours before I was scheduled to leave for the airport. Then, after a blissful final few hours in The Bed That Changed Everything, I was off to the airport to catch my next flight.

THE HEALING LOVE OF A TRUE FRIEND

From Istanbul, I had another brief transit stop in Amsterdam. I didn't receive a prompt this time to ask the gate agent if my bags were properly transferred, but I did it anyway. She said yes, but she either lied or didn't check thoroughly because my luggage had been left in Amsterdam. Again! Yep, only one bag showed up in Toronto with me eight hours later. Still, I didn't let this phase me because I was about to see one of my favorite people in the whole world. She used to be my boss—the best one I ever had, bar none. As a member of her team, she taught me new standards of excellence and business principles that still serve me today. Some people labeled her a tyrant and talked about her in disparaging terms. But for me, she stood as a model of a woman in business who takes strong, principled positions, doesn't apologize for them, and isn't afraid to make and execute tough decisions.

By the time I arrived in Toronto for the next leg of my Epic Trip, our boss-employee relationship was years in the past, and we'd been friends for about as long. I bedded down in her guest room. After The Bed That Changed Everything in Istanbul, her guest room bed was the next bed to elevate my bedding standards.

My friend and I played tourist in Toronto for a week and a half. We went indoor skydiving—laughing the whole time at how terrible we were at it—visited Ripley's Aquarium, did at-home facials, and went to church.

My missing luggage finally caught up with me the night before we headed out to Niagara Falls. After an easy drive of a couple of hours, we spent the afternoon wandering the streets and the evening at a wax museum.

The next morning, my friend and I donned ponchos and got on a boat heading for the falls. In less than thirty minutes on that boat, we felt like we had the thrill of our lives—keeping our balance as the boat bobbed through the rough water, feeling the refreshing spray on our faces, delighting in the power of the water roaring over the falls, and the beauty of the scene before us made it so.

We drove back to Toronto that afternoon, relaxed but still in tourist mode. Over the next few days, we took in a Toronto Blue Jays baseball game at Rogers Centre, visited the CN Tower, and went on a wine-tasting excursion. Then, just like that, our week and a half together was over.

My friend showered me with love for a week and a half. Yes, we visited lots of places together, but as much fun as we had, it wasn't the going out that made our time together special. It was her making me warm milk every night so I'd sleep well. It was our heart-to-heart talk on her deck one sunny morning over our steaming mugs of hot chocolate and coffee. And it was the quiet moments when we simply enjoyed being in each other's company. God used my friend as His hands, feet, and heart, and I unbroke just a little more as she poured her love into me.

NATURAL WONDERS

After a week and a half of loving on me, my friend saw me off at the Toronto airport. I was heading west to Vancouver to board my Alaskan cruise.

As a kid, I loved watching *The Love Boat* on TV but didn't aspire to go on a cruise. Still, this seemed like the most efficient way to fulfill my dream of visiting Alaska. To say I was overcome with excitement as I took my first step onto the deck of the cruise ship would be an understatement. The buzz emanating from me could have powered the ship all the way to the Arctic Ocean.

I left my luggage, which didn't get left behind this time, in my cabin and headed out to explore the ship. I found the restaurants, gym, spa, and entertainment areas. Then I showered, dressed for dinner, and went back to the gym, where I won a drawing for a free spa treatment. It was a wonderful beginning to what was a pretty perfect seven days.

After dinner, I strolled around the deck with a big grin on my face because I was finally on my way to Alaska.

The next morning, I enjoyed my first Alaskan sunrise as I power-walked around the deck. I didn't care that I was probably the youngest person on deck at that time of the day. I was too stoked to stay tucked up in bed.

Of the seven days we would be cruising, we had three ports of call, and I had pre-booked all my shore excursions. So, after my early morning walk, I got ready for the day, had breakfast, and disembarked. We had docked in Ketchikan, where I joined other cruisers for a nature walk through a rainforest on a nearby island. I was in heaven as the island's beauty, quiet, and peace filled my wellspring of joy.

The next day, we docked in Juneau, and I went off to enjoy an easy hike to Mendenhall Glacier, my first real-life glacier. The hike was beautiful, but the glacier blew my mind. The magnitude of what I was seeing—ice that had taken hundreds of years to flow from its source in the mountains down to Mendenhall Lake—made me feel like I was back in the Serengeti. It was a less intense experience but somehow just as powerful. God's awesome creation surrounded and pressed in on me, filling me with joy. The day couldn't have been more perfect, and contentment seeped from my pores as I drifted off to sleep in my cabin back onboard the ship that night.

NATURE'S HEALING

For the entire seven days of the cruise, I spent every departure on deck watching the place we were leaving disappear behind us and looking forward to our next port of call. As long as I was awake when we arrived at our next port, I also watched as the ship docked. So, I was watching with avid interest as we pulled into port in Skagway, Alaska. I'd never heard of the town before I started making my cruise arrangements, but I was looking forward to my shore excursion, which was a train ride up a mountain near the Canadian border. With my love of trains *and* mountains, you can imagine how excited I was.

The train ride did not disappoint. I spent the entire two hours of the excursion hanging over the railing of a platform between two train cars, snapping photos of the mountain, the matchstick bridges we crossed, and the town way down below. I kept telling myself to stop and sit inside for a while, but I couldn't. It was too mesmerizing. Sure, it was chilly on the uncovered platform, but my joy and exhilaration warmed me from the inside out.

After the train excursion was over, I wandered around the town for a while, buying a few souvenirs and enjoying the afterglow from the experience I'd just had. Back on the ship, I had lunch and enjoyed the Swedish massage that I'd won on the first day of the cruise.

Ketchikan had been lovely, Juneau had been wonderful, Skagway had been brilliant, and I didn't expect the cruise to keep getting better. But oh, how it did as we cruised Glacier Bay for the next two days! I spent the entire first day in Glacier Bay on the ship's top deck—bouncing from side to side and from front to back, whatever it took to get the best views—absorbing nature's beauty and majesty. Sure, it was cold on deck, and I had to dash back to my cabin a couple of times to add more layers of clothes. But the wonder of the cold beauty in front of me kept healing my heart and filling me with joy.

NEW POSSIBILITIES

If I thought the first day cruising Glacier Bay was great, the next day was straight-up phenomenal. We cruised right up to Hubbard Glacier, the largest freshwater glacier in North America. It's about seven miles wide at the shoreline, where the ice is around four hundred years old. This means the ice had started its journey from the glacier's source four hundred years earlier and, with a thunderous crack, I watched that baby calve. Twice. Brand-new icebergs broke off Hubbard Glacier while I watched. Twice!

I was in indescribable bliss—the kind I only experience in God's awesome, mind-blowing nature. I had never even known to imagine this, and now, I was living it.

Eventually, our captain executed a beautiful turn, and I watched from the back of the ship as the superb Hubbard Glacier disappeared behind us. Our two days in Glacier Bay had changed me yet again.

I had experienced even more new wonders, and my mind had continued to expand beyond the small box of my previous existence. Those two days opened my mind to possibilities that, two years later, led to five phenomenal years of living near the Arctic Circle.

Getting out into the world—*doing* things instead of *wishing* I was doing them—was changing me from the inside out. Not only was it healing the broken parts of me, but it was also opening me up to new possibilities and desires.

My Epic Trip was coaxing the kernel of my dream that God had given me as a child to explore the world—the same dream I'd let others disparage, the same one I'd buried under a pile of shame—into a budding flower and nothing could stop me now.

On the last night of the cruise, I went to bed beyond satisfied. As far as I was concerned, my Epic Trip was over and I needed nothing else.

BEAUTY AND MAJESTY

Eight days after I walked onto the cruise ship in Vancouver, British Columbia, I disembarked in Seward, Alaska. The rising sun was just starting to paint the sky pink and orange when I boarded a scenic cruise train from Seward for a five-hour ride to Anchorage.

As it had been after three dusty safari days, my hair was a hot mess, and I did not care. I only cared about the seven magnificent days I had just lived through. They represented my unrealistic, unattainable, impossible, God-given dreams coming true.

For the journey to Anchorage, I figured I'd relax on the train and read or chat with my fellow seatmates. And I tried—boy, did I try—but I was happy to fail. With the ceiling of the train car and half of its wall made of glass, our eyes were treated to the stunning wilds of Alaska. I should have been content snuggled down in the warmth and comfort inside the train car, but nothing beats being as close to the view as possible. So, as I had in Skagway, I spent most of the ride hanging over the side of the uncovered platform as we passed by marvelous glaciers, alongside gorgeous meadows, over babbling streams, and next to glassy lakes. I repeatedly forced myself back inside the car to warm up, but I couldn't stay seated. Within minutes, I'd pop up again and head back out onto the platform to take in the scene with nothing between it and my eyes. Why should I stay inside with all that beauty and majesty just outside?

I truly couldn't have orchestrated a better ending to my cruise.

THE PLACE WHERE HE INCREASES

From beginning to end, I loved my Alaskan adventure because, following my unforgettable Tanzanian safari, I met God again out there. We know that God is everywhere, and we can meet Him any time we want, but I find that my God-awareness and willingness to decrease so He can increase in my life intensifies whenever I spend time in wild, uninhabited nature.

Whether it's camping, hiking, or cruising by glaciers, I meet God in a different way in nature. It humbles me, pries my grasping fingers off my need for control, and invites me to surrender myself to Him all over again.

From Anchorage, I flew to New York, where I spent the next week with family, reestablishing old bonds and forming new ones. Although I'd been traveling to New York since I was six years old, this was my first time visiting it as an intentional tourist. So, as I had in every place I'd visited since I set out on my Epic Trip, I hit the streets and walked through recent and distant American history.

I visited the 9/11 Memorial, where I cried as I made my way through the exhibits, reliving my own memories of that tragic time. I also got on a ferry bound for the Statue of Liberty and Ellis Island, which I'd never visited before but whose histories I thoroughly enjoyed learning. For the rest of my time in New York, I visited a few other fairly forgettable landmarks, ran some errands, went to a barbecue, and relaxed. Before I knew it, my Epic Trip was over, and it was time to return to Jamaica.

Looking back now, I see my week in New York as a time of transition. It was a time to slow down as I switched gears from the monumental experiences of the previous two months to the ordinary reality of my life in Jamaica, where I still had no job and no idea what to do next.

Over the two months of my Epic Trip, God increased in my life, and I decreased in my vanity, my pride, and the lie that I knew it all. God had used His creation and the love of my friends to unbreak my heart, to humble me, and to get me ready for His next move in my life.

A DIFFERENT WOMAN

By any measure, my Epic Trip of 2015 was a roaring success. I ate, prayed, and loved my way through three continents, five countries, and fourteen cities. I slept in eleven beds and traveled on sixteen flights, three boats, one ship, and two trains. I rode on countless trams, buses, and subways, in several cars, and in one bajaj. I also experienced phenomenal firsts—my first safari, my first gourmet meal, my first glacier, and my first cruise, to name a few.

Kristine Bolt

I believe the entire trip was a gift from God meant to nourish my body, soul, and heart, to show me that the dream He'd given me was possible, and to set me up for the adventures and opportunities He had in store for me.

I returned to Jamaica a completely different woman from the one who had left there two months earlier. I returned with a mostly healed heart and brand-new perspectives. I returned feeling better and more whole than ever, and I knew I couldn't stop my journey now.

My Epic Trip turned out to be far more than a trip. It opened my eyes, mind, and heart in unexpected and sometimes inexplicable ways. It started opening me up to possibilities that made embracing an ordinary life again impossible. God used it to show me that dreaming big—huge, even—is scary but necessary because the moments when those dreams become real are the moments when I remember His awesome power. He used my Epic Trip to show me what could be.

9

A WHOLE NEW WORLD

Jesus looked at them intently and said, "Humanly speaking, it is impossible. But with God everything is possible." Matthew 19:26 ESV

From my quiet desperation and unfulfillment in my misery-soaked life through my tumble to rock bottom, from God's grace in extending His hand of rescue to me through unbreaking me on my Epic Trip, a whole new world opened up right before my very eyes. As I reflected on it, several lessons for the unhappy, unfulfilled woman I used to be have became crystal clear.

Oh, how much less misery I would have tolerated, how much less time I would have stayed stuck, and how much stronger my faith would have been if someone had taught me these lessons. But no one did, which is exactly why I'm sharing them now with you.

The details of your story may be different from mine, but it's no less riddled with feelings of disappointment, rejection, abandonment, dissatisfaction, despair, or unworthiness. Take these lessons, chew on them, digest them, and let the

Holy Spirit use them to unbreak you and set you free. Let Him use these lessons to open your eyes and heart to a whole new world.

LESSON 1: LET GOD BE GOD

As far back as I can remember, I dreamed of a traveling lifestyle. But back then, the only people I knew who lived the way I wanted to were National Geographic crews, diplomats, and international development professionals. They were the elite few, and no amount of wishing or trying helped me to break into their ranks. On top of my efforts to get into these fields turning out to be futile, I let the world scoff at my dream and shame me into burying it.

I see now that my lack of confidence in myself and my lack of faith and trust in God made it easy for me to swallow the world's lie that the dream God gave me was stupid and impossible. Imagine my surprise when I discovered the exact opposite to be true!

I've learned that I need to trust in Him, commit to the dream, and practice patient endurance to see it through. As a result, I've lived dreams I didn't even know to dream.

I've also learned that the path I thought was the only one that could lead me to realize my dream wasn't what God had planned for me. As I sat in my parents' guest room trying to decide on a new career direction, I thought international development had to be it since I wanted to see the world and help people while doing it. But God had a whole other plan in the works and, as a result, He kept the door to international development firmly shut against me.

You see, the more you take the limits off God, get in sync with Him, and learn to keep your heart tuned and eyes peeled for your next God-ordained move, the more you'll be amazed at what He can do with the seed He's planted in you.

From Southeast Asia to Siberia, from East Africa to Alaska, every journey I've taken since God started unbreaking me and healing my heart has transformed me into the woman He always meant for me to be. More importantly, every transformation has been a story that blesses other women. Isn't it amazing what God can do with one silly-looking dream?

So know this: the thing God has planted in you to do—no matter how impossible, insignificant, or trivial it looks to the rest of the world—has the power to change lives: yours and others'.

LESSON 2: EMBRACE THE DISCOMFORT OF CHANGE

Most humans hate change. We may say we welcome it, but we're mostly deceiving ourselves with that claim.

In general, people resist and fear change because they prefer familiar situations—even ones they claim to hate—over unfamiliar situations. But growth only comes through change, even as confusing, heartbreaking, or uncontrollable as it can feel.

Change forces you to try something different, which causes you to grow beyond your self-imposed boundaries into someone you never thought you could be. Change opens up the opportunity for you to expand how you see yourself.

In my old life, my goal was to acquire the things the world said would make me feel successful. Well, I did—I got it all, but none of it fulfilled me. Only when I surrendered to God and stopped trying to go my own way did I finally find the fulfillment I so desperately craved and the freedom to live the life God always had for me.

These days, my goal is to squeeze every ounce of God-given potential out of every day I live. I want to enjoy as much as possible, impact as many as possible, and achieve as much as possible. Without change, none of that can happen. Without change, I would settle into my routine and stop challenging or pushing myself beyond where I'm comfortable. I would keep missing all that God has for me.

Change also requires you to let go of dead things—dead seasons, dead relationships, and dead stuff. I clung to my hated corporate job, my toxic relationship, and my ill-fitting lifestyle because I feared letting them go, even though they were bringing nothing but death to my soul. I thought that because those were the things I'd chosen, I had to keep choosing them. But not everything or everyone is in your life forever. Some things and people are with you for a season, and it's okay to let them go when that season is over.

As I learned firsthand, and as you probably know through harsh experience, hanging on to things and people whose time has passed can be counterproductive or even painful. Plus, clinging to dead things causes you to miss new opportunities God sends your way.

If I had kept clinging to the dead job, dead relationships, and dead stuff I owned, I would never have summitted Mt. Kilimanjaro six months after first seeing it. I would never have gone dogsledding through a pristine, snow-laden Siberian forest three years after God liberated me from my old life. And I surely would never have expanded my mind through learning new languages, trying new cuisines, or embarking on several new careers.

If not for change and letting go of dead things, I wouldn't have walked away from the world's plan for me and into God's awesome plan for my life.

LESSON 3: DISCOVER THE TRUE YOU

As I was on my slide to rock bottom, I let my ex convince me that I was "not enough" of this or "too much" of that. I was never just right as I was, and I let his destructive, wrong opinions rob me of my identity in Christ and my confidence in myself. As I absorbed his lies, I thought it wasn't okay to be me. So I hid myself—my true thoughts, feelings, dreams, and desires—and sank deeper into fear and fakeness.

My Epic Trip of 2015 was my first step in reestablishing my identity and getting my confidence and courage back. It started teaching me to rely on God—for approval, direction, or anything else I need—instead of looking to others or myself as my source. It started teaching me the joy of being whole and complete in Christ instead of looking for someone else to complete me. It even elevated my passport to the status of my most prized possession. As much as I love to look great, no cute shoes, fabulous outfits, or gorgeous accessories have a prayer of coming close.

My Epic Trip helped me to start reorganizing my priorities as I began to see myself as the fearfully and wonderfully made woman God created me to be.

I've also learned that every unapologetic step you take to become more of who God made you to be is priceless for restoring your confidence and building your courage. Plus, as you re-root your identity in Christ and get your confidence back, people's judgments don't matter as much anymore because you know who you are, the Source of your strength, and what you can do…with God.

LESSON 4: ELEVATE THE MOST IMPORTANT RELATIONSHIP

As God put the broken pieces of my heart back together again, I reestablished my identity and my confidence in myself. But more importantly, I established a deeper confidence in Jesus as my Savior, God as my loving Father, and the Holy Spirit as my ever-present Companion.

I know firsthand what it's like to be in God's presence because I've felt it—first as Dearson and I drove up Ngorongoro Crater, and a few months later, during my grueling climb up Mt. Kilimanjaro. I know He's always with me because I've seen it. And, despite my years of thinking He had me on mute, I know He always hears me. Sometimes it may seem like He doesn't answer me immediately, but now I know He loves me too much to ever ignore me.

I no longer stare out windows wondering what all my striving is for because now I'm a woman rooted in purpose. Yes, I still weep in praise and worship, but now it's from joy and gratitude for how far God has brought me from the outwardly happy-looking but secretly unfulfilled, miserable, stuck woman I used to be.

Through it all, no matter what's happening around or in me—blocked paths, closed doors, seemingly unscalable mountains, fickle feelings, or the death of a relationship—my faith in God grows and deepens. And I wouldn't trade this journey of trust, freedom, and fulfillment for anything.

10

FREEDOM

Christ has set us free to live a free life. So take your stand!
Never again let anyone put a harness of slavery on you.
Galatians 5:1 MSG

I wrote the story of how God unbroke me because of a terrible speech delivered to a group of twenty-something-year-old service club members. I wrote the story of how God saved me from the pit of a life I'd created for myself as a do-over of that terrible speech.

Unlike that speech, this book isn't about the wonderful things I did and experienced as I allowed God to start healing me. Instead, it's my way of sharing with you God's amazing grace and the freedom I discovered in Christ: freedom from condemnation, freedom from fear of others' opinions and judgments, freedom from unfulfillment, and freedom from misery day in and day out.

My darling, God's gift of freedom isn't only for me; it's for you too. He wants to save you. He wants to heal your broken heart and use new experiences to transform you into the woman He created you to be. If you let Him, He'll make you free in ways you can't even imagine now, and He'll open your eyes to worlds you don't even know exist.

Your path will be different from mine because the dreams and desires God planted in you are different from the ones He planted in me. It will be different because your pain, baggage, and trauma from the past are different from mine. But as you let Him lead you, step by step, on the path to making those dreams and desires real, He'll unbreak you, heal your heart, free you from your self-imposed chains, and change your life—just as He did for me and for every other Christian woman who surrenders her entire life and being to Him.

Won't you trust Him now?

YOUR NEXT STEPS

As you read this book, you relived the most pivotal time in my life with me. Through its pages, you journeyed with me over a span of about nine months as I went through sudden, sweeping, all-at-once changes that shattered me and demolished the life I'd created. Then you watched as I spent months letting God put me back together again and turn me in a new direction.

You saw how I broke myself and how God unbroke me, and you peeked in on the lessons I learned during that season. Yes, it was my story, but it can be your story too, even if not in the way you think.

This isn't about you dropping everything, saying sayonara to the haters, and heading off for a two-month, around-the-world, eat-pray-love journey. It's about you digging up the seed God planted in you instead of burying it under shame or regret. It's about you abandoning your idols and turning back to God in repentance. And it's about accepting the freedom Jesus died to give you—freedom from sin, freedom from fear, freedom from death, and freedom from your self-imposed limits.

So here's what to do now.

STEP 1: TELL YOURSELF THE TRUTH

A big part of my misery in my old life came from not being truthful with myself about what I wanted. In fact, I buried what I wanted so far down in my consciousness that, in the depths of my misery, I didn't even know what I wanted anymore. I just knew that what I had wasn't it. I may have saved myself untold years of misery by telling myself the truth about the life I wanted to live.

So, your first step is to get honest with yourself and God about what you want. You can ask God what He wants of you and go from there, but if you've lost touch with your dreams, here's how to start resurrecting them. Get alone somewhere, close your eyes, release your self-judgment, and let yourself imagine that the slate of your life got wiped clean. You lost your job, your relationship broke up, and no one is depending on you for anything. You're free as a bird to make any decision you want. What or where would your first instinct lead you to? A whole new career direction? A whole new city or country? Maybe even a whole new you?

Give your imagination wings and allow yourself to simply dream your dreams.

STEP 2: PREPARE TO BE BRAVE

I let the world shame me into burying my dreams because I wasn't brave enough to stand by them, no matter how silly they seemed to others. My lack of courage led me to create a life that looked great on the outside but felt like a prison on the inside.

So, your next step is to pray and gather your courage to choose God's will over yours or anyone else's. This is where you decide on purpose whose opinion matters the most to you: other people's or God's.

I suggest writing down the names of every single person you fear would be disappointed in you, turn up their nose at you, shun you, or ridicule you because you decided to start going after your God-given dreams. Write every single name, then ask yourself if the consequences of their disappointment and disapproval are more important than the freedom and fulfillment God has for you.

STEP 3: GET QUIET AND LISTEN

It's easy to forget that prayer is a two-way street. I sure did! While praying for God to save me from my quagmire of a life, I never stopped to listen to what He may have been saying to me. Only after I was out of my mess did I realize that He'd sent answers to my prayers all along. But I missed them because I wasn't paying attention.

So once you have a handle on what you truly want—and what God wants of you—you'll need to tune in to the Holy Spirit to brainstorm your next best step in walking out God's will.

It's okay if your next step is small or if you're unsure of how it will get you to your dream. When I set off on my Epic Trip, I didn't know it would lead to the destruction of the boundaries I'd placed on myself. I also didn't know it would open up a whole new world of possibilities and later lead to new careers I never considered—including becoming an author.

Once you've taken these three steps, you'll need to do one more courageous thing: let go of what you have been clinging to. Whatever it is may look amazing, but if it's the thing that's making you wonder, "Why do I feel so unfulfilled?" then it may not be what God meant for you. Or it may be time to let go of parts of it that God wants you to move on from.

You see, you can't grab hold of the new things God wants to do in your life while you are desperately clinging to the old.

> *But forget all that—it is nothing compared to what I am going to do. Isaiah 43:18 NLT*

My darling, your future is bright, and God has more fulfillment and freedom for you than you can imagine. All you have to do is open your arms and receive it.

INDIVIDUAL REFLECTION OR BOOK CLUB DISCUSSION QUESTIONS

I hope you found the story of my journey from feeling unfulfilled to finding true freedom interesting. However, it's not solely for entertainment. I hope you can see some aspect of yourself or your life in it.

To help you do this, over the next few pages, you'll find questions covering each section of each chapter in this book. You can use these questions for private, individual reflection or as prompts for book club discussions if you're reading along with friends.

IN THE VALLEY OF DISCONTENT AND DESPAIR

1. What are your memories of feeling special to God?
2. If you've stopped feeling special to Him, when did that happen? How did it happen?
3. If you still feel special to Him, how have you kept that special feeling?

THE TRUTH UNDER THE LIE

1. What secret misery is hiding behind the mask of your great-looking life?

2. What have you done to try to solve the problem of your discontent and unfulfillment?
3. What have been the results of the things you've tried to solve the problem of your discontent and unfulfillment?

TRAPPED BY IDOLS

1. What have you set up as an idol or as idols in your life?
2. What are you looking to for fulfillment and satisfaction?
3. What is causing you to feel trapped in the life you've created?

THE SHADOW I BECAME

1. Who or what has destroyed your self-image and self-worth?
2. What's draining your joy, peace, and contentment from you that you're unwilling to let go of or walk away from because of the time and/or money you've invested in it?
3. What in your life are you being willfully blind to that you know isn't God's will or His best for you?

MISERY-RIDDLED TREASURE HOARDS

1. Which part or parts of your life look beautiful on the outside but tell a different story on the inside?

2. What is God calling you to let go of? Why are you afraid to let go of it?
3. What do you think God would have for you if you released your grip on what you're hanging on to and opened your hands to receive it?

THE SLIDE TO ROCK BOTTOM

1. What prayers have you prayed that seem to be unanswered by God? How do you feel about that?
2. What is it that you want God to do for you?
3. In what ways have you felt rejected by people? How may God use that rejection for His glory?

THE DESCENT BEGINS

1. How do you feel about God acting in your life to free you in ways you would never expect?
2. The price that God requires for your freedom may be you releasing your idols—the things that are causing you to feel stuck or trapped. Would you be willing to pay that price? Why or why not?
3. What does freedom mean to you? What does it look, feel, smell, sound, and taste like?

THE GIRL I USED TO BE

1. In what ways have you sold yourself short or lowered your standards to make what you're clinging to feel acceptable?

2. Think about the thing you're clinging to the tightest. Ask and answer the question: "What if God has something better for me?"
3. What would rock bottom look like for you?
4. What would you have to let go of to let God rescue you from your misery before you slide all the way to rock bottom?

THE PEACE OF GOD (AND A WHOLE LOT MORE)

1. How may God be using someone else's hardened heart as a setup to work miracles and wonders in your life?
2. What would it take for you to truly believe that God never ignores you and that He always has your back?
3. If fear wasn't a factor, how would you feel about starting your life fresh with God?

STRIPPED BARE

1. What emotions would you feel if you had to, or got to, start your life all over again? Why would you feel this way?
2. Imagine that you could restart your life tomorrow. What would you do differently?
3. How may God already be working in unexpected ways in your life to get your attention so He can rescue you from your dissatisfaction or misery?

THE GIFT OF SALVATION

1. What are the things and who are the people that you've been using to fill the God-sized hole in your heart?
2. What do you think God may be waiting for you to let go of so you can grab onto His gift of true salvation?
3. What if you don't have to wait until you hit rock bottom to choose God's way? What if you can just decide to do it now?

WHO ARE YOU?

1. Behind the masks that you wear and the roles that you play, who are you really?
2. If the things you own and the positions you hold were taken away from you, who would be left? Who would you be then?
3. How do you feel about the answers you've given or couldn't give?

HITTING RESET

1. What have you always dreamed of being or doing?
2. What's stopped you from being or doing it?
3. Imagine you could restart your life and people's opinions didn't matter. What possibilities does God reveal to you?

THE RESURRECTION OF THE DEAD

1. In what area or areas of your life have you taken control away from God out of impatience or a lack of trust?
2. What's the world's definition of success that you've taken as your own?
3. What's God's definition of success for you?
4. What standards does God have for you that you've abandoned in favor of the world's standards?

A SILLY, FRIVOLOUS DREAM

1. What dream have you given up on because it felt too hard?
2. In what ways have you let the world trample on the dream God placed in your heart?
3. What would you do if you believed that your beautiful, neglected, God-given dream wasn't stupid, trivial, or far-fetched?
4. What if your hidden, most precious, burning desire is a seed that God planted to direct you to His purpose for your life?

A GOD-GIVEN, LIFE-CHANGING DREAM

1. Would you still be willing to go after the dream God gave you if you were the only one who believed in it? Why or why not?
2. What do you imagine your life would look like if you chose to go after the dream God gave you, no matter

what? What would be different? What would be the same?

3. Imagine you've taken the next step God set before you that will take you towards your dream. What emotions do you feel? Why?

GET UP AND GO

1. What have you been talking about seeing or doing that you haven't seen or done?
2. What's stopping you from doing the things you dream of doing or going to the places you dream of going to?
3. What one small thing can you do that's directly related to the dream God placed in your heart?

FALLING IN LOVE

1. How might indulging in an activity you love or have dreamed of doing counteract the misery, unfulfillment or darkness permeating your life?
2. What's stopping you from exploring new settings or activities as possible new sources of love in your life?
3. What if it's okay that your first step towards the dream God has given you doesn't look like it serves or benefits anyone but you?

BREAKING OLD BOUNDARIES

1. What are all the things you think are holding you back from expanding beyond the limits of your

current existence? What emotions are stopping you from pushing those limits?

2. How willing are you to let God expand you beyond your comfort zone?
3. In what ways can you uplevel how you care for, move, and use your body?
4. In what ways can you let God use your body to expand your mind?

HEALING WONDERS

1. In what ways do you think being out in nature can help heal your heart and soothe your soul?
2. God used nature to start unbreaking me. What do you think God can use to unbreak you?

"I LOVE YOU"

1. To what locations or settings do you find yourself drawn so you can feel closer to God?
2. If God were to write you a love letter, what do you imagine it would say?
3. If you were to write a love letter to God, what would you say?

UNBREAK ME

1. What darkness is lingering in your heart, stealing the light of the beauty surrounding you?
2. What's standing in the way of you forgiving the hurts in your heart?

3. What if—on the other side of forgiveness—peace and contentment like you can't begin to imagine are waiting for you? Would you be willing to forgive the hurts in your heart then?

A POSTCARD FROM GOD

1. Do you want to be a different woman when you go to bed tonight than the woman you woke up as this morning? If yes, in what way? If not, why not?
2. Think back on your day yesterday. In retrospect, what opportunities can you see that God gave you to be more of the woman He created you to be? How did you handle those opportunities?
3. God is inviting you to lay your burdens down right now. Will you? Why or why not?

THE BIG FIVE

1. God's Big Five for you in this season are love, joy, peace, trust, and faith. How can you invite more of each of these into your current situation?
2. How could more love, joy, peace, trust, and faith impact how you feel about, show up for, and make decisions in your life right now?

THE PRESENCE OF GOD

1. What does intimacy with God look like for you?

2. What are all the factors—people, situations, or emotions—stopping you from drawing closer to God?

3. For each person, situation, or emotion stopping you from drawing closer to God, ask yourself and answer, "Why is this not a good enough reason for me to keep God at a distance?"

A LESSON ON OFFENSE

1. Think of an offense about which you're still sore. How can you reframe the circumstances so you drop your feeling of offense?

2. If the situation should ever reoccur, how could you skip feeling offended this time?

3. How may your unforgiveness over these offenses be standing in the way of God's best for you?

4. Which do you want more—your feelings of offense and unforgiveness or God's abundant blessings?

HEALING, HEALING, AND MORE HEALING

1. What may God be trying to use to heal your heart that you haven't noticed before now?

2. What may God be trying to use to heal your body that you haven't noticed before now?

3. What may God be trying to use to renew your mind that you haven't noticed before now?

LEARNING TO LISTEN AND OBEY

1. What are some of the seen and unseen consequences of dismissing the Holy Spirit's promptings in your life?

2. Think of the last time you felt a strong prompting to take an action but dismissed it. What consequences—small or large, seen or unseen—can you see now that came about as a result?

ANOTHER NEW STANDARD

1. In what areas of your life is God prompting you to come up higher in your expectations, standards, or behavior?

2. How would your life be different if you took up God's charge to come up higher in these areas?

THE HEALING LOVE OF A TRUE FRIEND

1. In what ways can you be a friend who is God's hands, feet, and heart of love to others?

2. Over this past week, where did you miss opportunities to be God's hands, feet, and heart for others?

3. Over the coming week, how can you become more alert to opportunities to be God's hands, feet, and heart for others?

NATURAL WONDERS

1. Being out in nature in high places or cold places helps heal and reset me and refills my wellspring of joy. What part of God's creation does the same for you?
2. If you don't know what part of God's creation helps to heal, reset, and refill you, how can you find out?

NATURE'S HEALING

1. What's the biggest thing weighing you down or keeping you stuck in pain?
2. What may God be trying to use as a healing balm for past hurts that you've resisted or haven't noticed?
3. Do you want to be set free from what's weighing you down or keeping you stuck? If yes, why? If not, why not? Keep asking and answering, "Why?" until you get to the real truth.

NEW POSSIBILITIES

1. What are you feeding your mind through your eyes and ears—through what you watch, read, and listen to?
2. What activities and sources can you use to fill your body with wonder, belief, and light?
3. What activities and sources do you need to eliminate because they make your body a dark, dank cellar?

BEAUTY AND MAJESTY

1. Psalm 96:6 says that honor and majesty surround God. What does this mean to you?
2. What aspects of God's beauty and majesty do you notice in your everyday life?

THE PLACE WHERE HE INCREASES

1. In what area is God calling you to decrease so He can increase in your life?
2. Are you willing to decrease and let God increase in your life? Why or why not?

A DIFFERENT WOMAN

1. One of the things God uses to grow and transform me is travel. What does He use in your life?
2. How has God tried to transform and grow you over the past twelve months? How have you resisted or missed Him?
3. What do you think would be possible in your life if you allowed God to transform you into the woman He created you to be?

LESSON 1: LET GOD BE GOD

1. Who could you impact and influence for the better if you took the next step God has for you, no matter what?

2. What one simple step can you take towards a dream God has given you?

LESSON 2: EMBRACE THE DISCOMFORT OF CHANGE

1. What dead things—seasons, relationships, or stuff—is God calling you to let go of?
2. Why do you think you're afraid to let go of the dead things in your life? As you answer, probe deeper by asking, "But why?" Don't stop until you uncover the real reason.

LESSON 3: DISCOVER THE TRUE YOU

1. On what foundation have you built your identity? On other people's opinions of you? On what the world says you should do or be? Or on who God says you are?
2. Who does God say you are?

LESSON 4: ELEVATE THE MOST IMPORTANT RELATIONSHIP

1. Who are Jesus, God, and the Holy Spirit to you?
2. What active role does each member of the Trinity play in your life?
3. What do you truly believe about God's constancy and reliability?

FREEDOM

1. Where do you feel the most stuck or in bondage right now?
2. What does freedom look like for you in this area?
3. Do you trust in God and His plan for you to live free? Why or why not?

YOUR NEXT STEPS

1. What if it turns out that what you want isn't what God has for you? Will you still be all-in with Him? Why or why not?
2. There is no such thing as not enough time. There is only time we make for what we want to do and what's important to us. Will you set time aside to take the three steps I laid out in this book? Why or why not?

ABOUT THE AUTHOR

Kristine Bolt is an author, blogger, world traveler, and champion of possibilities. She spent 16+ years in the corporate world, where she accumulated heaps of business experience. Meanwhile, she also lost sight of her God-given dream and lost faith in the possibility of ever living it. In recent years, she's written and spoken extensively on discovering your God-given calling and the freedom to walk it out. Her passion is helping women go from feeling stuck and trapped in misery and unfulfillment to believing in the possibility of their God-given dreams so they can take their next step with courage and confidence.

Kris blogs at kristinebolt.com.

THANK YOU FOR READING!

I appreciate your feedback and I love hearing what you have to say. So, I'd like to ask for a super quick favor.

Can you take two minutes to leave an honest review of this book on Amazon?

Truly, it would mean the world to me. But more importantly, your review helps get this book in front of other women who need to know that they're not alone in feeling unfulfilled and dissatisfied in their lives.

So please leave a helpful review of this book on Amazon: kristinebolt.com/theunbrokenmereview.

Thanks a million.

Kris ♡♡

www.ingramcontent.com/pod-product-compliance
Lightning Source LLC
Chambersburg PA
CBHW060942040426
42445CB00011B/973